RAND NATIONAL DEFENSE RESEARCH INSTITUTE

Ensuring Language Capability in the Intelligence Community

What Factors Affect the Best Mix of Military, Civilians, and Contractors?

Beth J. Asch, John D. Winkler

Prepared for the Office of the Director of National Intelligence

Approved for public release; distribution unlimited

The research described in this report was prepared for the Office of the Director of National Intelligence. The research was conducted within the RAND National Defense Research Institute, a federally funded research and development center sponsored by the Office of the Secretary of Defense, the Joint Staff, the Unified Combatant Commands, the Navy, the Marine Corps, the defense agencies, and the defense Intelligence Community under Contract W74V8H-06-C-0002.

Library of Congress Cataloging-in-Publication Data is available for this publication.

ISBN: 978-0-8330-7784-4

The RAND Corporation is a nonprofit institution that helps improve policy and decisionmaking through research and analysis. RAND's publications do not necessarily reflect the opinions of its research clients and sponsors.

Support RAND—make a tax-deductible charitable contribution at
www.rand.org/giving/contribute.html

RAND® is a registered trademark.

Cover photo: iStockphoto/Thinkstock

© Copyright 2013 RAND Corporation

This document and trademark(s) contained herein are protected by law. This representation of RAND intellectual property is provided for noncommercial use only. Unauthorized posting of RAND documents to a non-RAND website is prohibited. RAND documents are protected under copyright law. Permission is given to duplicate this document for personal use only, as long as it is unaltered and complete. Permission is required from RAND to reproduce, or reuse in another form, any of our research documents for commercial use. For information on reprint and linking permissions, please see the RAND permissions page (www.rand.org/pubs/permissions.html).

RAND OFFICES
SANTA MONICA, CA • WASHINGTON, DC
PITTSBURGH, PA • NEW ORLEANS, LA • JACKSON, MS • BOSTON, MA
DOHA, QA • CAMBRIDGE, UK • BRUSSELS, BE

www.rand.org

Preface

Language capability is provided in the intelligence community by military personnel, government civilians, and contractors. A key question is what is the best mix of these three types of personnel in terms of cost and effectiveness. RAND was asked by the Chief Human Capital Office within the Office of the Director of National Intelligence to provide information to guide decisionmakers in their choice of workforce mix to provide language capability.

The research draws on U.S. Department of Defense guidance and the economics and management literatures to provide a framework for broadly assessing the costs and benefits of different sources of personnel to provide a given capability, including language capabilities. It then uses qualitative and quantitative approaches to identify the factors that may affect the best mix of language capability in the intelligence community. The qualitative approach involved taking a case-study approach and focusing on one agency, the National Security Agency/Central Security Service (NSA/CSS), and conducting extensive interviews throughout it. The quantitative approach involved developing a prototype model to compute the relative costs and benefits of different sources of personnel to provide language capability from a government-wide perspective. Both the qualitative and quantitative analyses are not definitive because they each have limitations, but they are complementary and provide some insights that could be considered in weighing the factors that could affect the best mix of language professionals in the intelligence community. Furthermore, the methods used and the insights gained could have broader applicability beyond language professionals.

This research should be of interest to people concerned about language capability in the intelligence community and those more broadly interested in analysis of the best mix of personnel to meet a given need in the national security context. The report assumes some knowledge about the federal civil service and military workforces and costing.

This research was sponsored by the Office of the Director of National Intelligence and conducted within the Intelligence Policy Center and the Forces and Resources Policy Center of RAND's National Defense Research Institute, a federally funded research and development center sponsored by the Office of the Secretary of Defense, the Joint Staff, the Unified Combatant Commands, the Navy, the Marine Corps, the defense agencies, and the defense Intelligence Community.

For more information on the RAND Intelligence Policy Center and on the Forces and Resources Policy Center, see http://www.rand.org/nsrd/ndri/centers/intel.html and http://www.rand.org/nsrd/ndri/centers/frp.html, or contact the respective director of each center (contact information is provided on the web pages).

Executive Summary

To provide language capability in the intelligence community, RAND analysis suggests that the Chief Human Capital Office in the Office of the Director of National Intelligence (ODNI) should continue to use language professionals from three personnel categories: military service members, government civilians, and contractors. The analysis indicates that each category of personnel provides unique advantages and belongs in the workforce mix. The analysis suggests that the intelligence community do the following:

- Build intelligence community language capability around permanent civilian positions.
- Continue to develop and train military personnel.
- Continue to use contractors to augment and extend the military and civilian workforce.

Several factors can inform the selection and management of language professionals. Existing U.S. Department of Defense (DoD) guidance directs that risk mitigation should take precedence over cost savings when necessary to maintain appropriate control of government operations and missions. If no such needs are present, then civilians are generally the preferred source of manpower. In addition, it is important to consider a time horizon sufficiently long enough to incorporate the career patterns of a variety of personnel. Finally, when assessing the costs and benefits of using personnel from different categories, it is useful to understand the factors that drive differences in productivity as well as labor costs. Productivity includes not just the amount of work performed but also quality, timeliness, and responsiveness, which are determined by knowledge, skills, and abilities; availability and flexibility; incentives; and other factors.

RAND used a case-study approach and conducted interviews at one critical agency that uses a large language workforce, the National Security Agency/Central Security Service. We also interviewed functional managers and language managers in DoD and ODNI, and we reviewed DoD workforce policy.

We supplemented the interviews with an exploratory, quantitative analysis of the relative cost and effectiveness of military versus government civilian language professionals from a government-wide perspective. The different analyses were consistent and complementary in reaching conclusions about key factors affecting the best mix of personnel to provide language capability, including the value of depth of knowledge and previous language experience. The exploratory analysis suggests that, from a government-wide perspective, civilians are a more cost-effective source of language capability than military personnel, even after accounting for the flow to the civil service of trained veterans with language capability. The key drivers of the higher cost of military personnel in the analysis are their high language-training costs, their relatively short careers, and the relatively low flow of trained veterans to the civil service, even though a large fraction of newly recruited civilians have prior military service. While the results are exploratory, they suggest that policies that reduce language-training costs and increase the flow of veterans to the civil service might be fruitful to consider further. It is important to recognize that considerations not included in the analysis also need to be weighed, such as the need for military-specific knowledge and skills and the ability to deploy and use military personnel in dangerous situations. Furthermore, results could differ with an agency-specific perspective.

In assessing workforce mix, RAND also made some observations about how to improve the management of military and civilian language professionals for the benefit of the defense and intelligence communities, drawing especially from the interviews RAND conducted. While additional analysis is needed to assess the feasibility and effectiveness of new policies, RAND recommends that the intelligence community consider assessment of the following:

- a career path for military language professionals that deviates from the typical enlisted career
- recruiting military personnel who are already proficient or nearly proficient in a foreign language
- incorporation into workforce mix decisions the additional contributions of civilian language professionals who are former military personnel, and steps to encourage the hiring of these language-proficient veterans
- current constraints on the hiring of civilians.

Contents

Figures and Tables

Figures

Tables

Summary

Language professionals play a pivotal role in U.S. national security. The adversaries of the United States communicate their plans and actions in many different languages and dialects. Consequently, U.S. intelligence operations require personnel with high-level capability in these languages and dialects. For example, in the area of signal intelligence, these professionals are required to listen to communications, decipher written and oral transmissions, and use and understand the colloquial phrases and syntax that are commonly used by native speakers of a language.

Language capability is provided in the intelligence community (IC) by military, government civilian, and contractor personnel. Each category of personnel offers different benefits for the IC—they have different capabilities, some cost more than others, and the IC is constrained in their use by different factors to varying degrees. A key question is, what is the best mix of these three categories of personnel in terms of cost and effectiveness to provide language capability? RAND was asked by the Chief Human Capital Office in the Office of the Director of National Intelligence (ODNI) to provide information to guide decisionmakers in their choice of workforce mix to provide language capability.

Approach

We applied both qualitative and quantitative methods to the study of the factors that could affect the optimum workforce mix to provide language capability in the IC. The qualitative approach involved taking a case-study approach and focusing on one critical agency that uses a large language workforce, the National Security Agency/Central Security Service (NSA/CSS), and conducting extensive interviews. First, however, we reviewed U.S. Department of Defense (DoD) workforce policy and guidance, which is relevant because our case study organization, NSA/CSS, is within DoD and because DoD policy can be a prototype for ODNI, which currently does not have policies for selecting the appropriate mix of military, civilian, and contractor personnel.

We also drew from the economics literature, the defense manpower literature and a recent DoD directive for information on the factors that drive the costs and benefits of different workforce mixes. Together with the DoD guidance, the information provides a framework for assessing workforce mix issues; we used this framework to develop the interview protocol we used for the interviews at the NSA/CSS, DoD, and ODNI. This qualitative analysis is especially informative about factors for which there are no data or for which measurement is problematic.

We supplemented the information we drew from the interviews with an exploratory, quantitative analysis of the relative cost and effectiveness of military versus nonveteran government civilian language professionals, taking a government-wide perspective. This perspective may differ from that of a single agency, because an individual agency may not bear the full cost or receive the full benefit of a given workforce mix decision. The analysis, also informed by the framework we developed, is exploratory because we were unable to gain access to NSA/CSS data on these personnel. Instead, we used multiple sources of information on the cost of military and civilian personnel to estimate costs and language proficiency. We conducted sensitivity analyses to assess to what extent our results might differ with data specific to the language community and with alternative assumptions, and we draw some insights on the factors affecting relative cost-effectiveness.

Because the data analysis is not specifically for the IC or for NSA/CSS language professionals, and the NSA/CSS case study focuses on one specific institution, our results should not be considered a definitive analysis of the best mix of language personnel at NSA/CSS or more broadly across the IC. Rather, they should guide further discussion and have broad applicability in other organizations and communities. That said, the qualitative and quantitative analysis provided complementary and consistent findings about the value of certain factors affecting the best mix of personnel, including experience and depth of knowledge.

A Framework for Assessing Workforce Mix and Management

DoD policy and our review of the literature identify several factors that can inform the selection and management of language professionals.

Risk Mitigation
DoD policy states that the workforce should be established to execute defense missions at a low to moderate level of risk and that risk mitigation should take precedence over cost savings when necessary to maintain appropriate control of government operations and missions. In general, government employees (civilian or military) are preferred over contractors, and military employees are preferred over civilians when military personnel are required for readiness or workforce needs. If no such needs are present, the guidance directs that civilians are the preferred source of manpower, unless a cost analysis indicates that they are relatively more costly.

A Long-Term Perspective on Costs and Benefits
At the request of the research sponsor, our analysis considered the overall costs to the government, rather than cost savings in a single organization or department, since the goal is to maximize the net return to taxpayer investment. Because agencies tend to consider only the costs and benefits of decisions to their own organization and not to other government organizations, implementing a government-wide perspective would require a change of policy and guidance on costing methodology in the IC. While such implementation strategies are important, they were beyond the scope of this study.

The time horizon must be long enough to incorporate the career patterns of a variety of personnel, because careers can differ significantly among different personnel types. For example, military personnel have shorter careers on average than government civilians, but have some chance of transitioning to the civilian or contractor workforce upon separation from the military. Consequently, a given number of military personnel may provide work years, and hence contribute to readiness in the intelligence community, well beyond those years provided while serving in uniform. Thus, the contribution of military personnel to mission readiness or accomplishment must incorporate the marginal value of their civilian career contributions. On the other hand, because civilians have longer careers and are more experienced, fewer civilians would be required to achieve a given level of readiness, and fewer civilian accessions would be needed to sustain a civilian force of a given size.

Productivity and the Factors That Drive Cost and Benefit

Our qualitative and quantitative analysis sought to gain information to guide policymakers about the best mix of language personnel in the IC. To that end, we sought information in the available literature on the drivers of the cost and benefits of different personnel categories and investigated, in our qualitative and quantitative analyses, whether these factors are important for language capability in the IC.

Differences in the benefits of using different personnel categories may stem from differences in productivity, and personnel with different productivity levels have different labor costs, at least theoretically. By productivity, we mean the array of ways personnel can contribute to readiness and effectiveness, which can include not just the amount of work performed but quality, timeliness, and responsiveness. Some of the factors that determine productivity, as identified in the literature, and therefore drive cost and benefit are knowledge, skills, and abilities; availability and flexibility; incentives; and miscellaneous factors. Knowledge, skills, and abilities can increase productivity as well as labor costs, and these, in turn, reflect training, education, heritage and ethnicity, and the amount and type of job experiences. Productivity also increases with work effort in response to performance incentives, as well as technology, the operational environment, and the type and extent of complementary skills. The availability of personnel and the flexibility to use personnel can vary by personnel type. For example, collateral duties may reduce availability by drawing away effort and attention, and different categories of personnel may have differing collateral duties.

Optimizing the Workforce Mix

The study provides—based on the qualitative and quantitative analysis, together with the framework we developed—broad guidance for decisionmakers on what factors policymakers might consider as they assess the optimum workforce mix to provide language capability. That said, our assessment indicates that there is also no simple rule of thumb for deciding workforce mix to provide language capability, because the missions to which personnel contribute are unique. Thus, while we offer some broad insights, each mission must be treated individually.

Use All Three Sources of Language Professionals for the Intelligence Community

The most important overarching observation of the study is that each category of personnel appears to provide unique advantages and belongs in the workforce mix.

Build the Intelligence Community's Language Capability Around Permanent Civilian Positions

There is a general perception, though by no means universal, that NSA/CSS needs more civilians providing language capability. Indeed, we were consistently told that civilians are the "backbone" of the language function in the IC—that they are more experienced and better educated, have greater language proficiency and deeper target knowledge, provide continuity, and bring other requisite capabilities, including writing and analytic skills and supervisory and mentoring capabilities. Furthermore, our exploratory modeling analysis provides complementary and consistent conclusions, suggesting that a workforce of civilian language professionals is relatively more cost-effective than a military one, from a government-wide perspective.

Much of the cost savings we estimate in the model stems from the fact that military personnel generally do not enter service with language proficiency and instead must be trained. The interviews indicate, past research shows, and the model assumes that enlisted personnel do not provide proficiency until the end of their second year. When the model allows enlisted personnel to provide language proficiency immediately, the relative cost advantage of civilians shrinks considerably. Thus, training adds substantially to the cost of military language personnel insofar as, in their initial years while they are being trained, they are costly but provide little or no proficiency to operational missions. The analysis suggests that, to the extent the armed services can recruit personnel who are already proficient or nearly proficient in needed languages, the cost of language capability provided by military personnel would decline and their cost-effectiveness relative to civilians would increase. However, recruiting military personnel may require more resources, and the cost of those resources must be factored into the cost analysis as well.

Of course, the cost of providing a given level of language proficiency is not the only consideration in weighing the benefits and costs of a military versus civilian workforce. Other considerations—including the need for military-specific knowledge and skills, the ability to deploy military personnel and use them in dangerous situations, and the benefits to the military that come from having some military personnel support strategic IC missions—can more than outweigh the relative costs we consider in the model. Furthermore, the results might differ if we were to take an agency-specific perspective rather than a government-wide perspective.

Continue to Invest in Development and Training of Military Personnel

Generally speaking, IC language missions should not be staffed only by civilians, though there will be specific instances where this is not true. Military personnel can bring unique knowledge, especially to missions requiring understanding of military tactics and the operational environment. Military personnel are generally young and in their first assignment, but they can be successfully mentored and developed over time. The Defense Language Institute Foreign Language Center (DLIFLC) is a unique resource that can provide a large and steady stream of trained language professionals to the IC. Our interviewees suggested that assignments at NSA/CSS also benefit the military by allowing military personnel to develop and use their language skills, providing them with a "big picture" of the national mission and, more pragmatically, a list of "who to call at NSA/CSS" when they return to their service mission and are in the field with questions.

Military personnel may also provide a "farm team" for the civilian workforce. Workforce mix analyses of military versus civilian personnel rarely account for the net contribution of the flow of military to civilian employment, and none of the DoD guidance indicates that it should be incorporated. Consequently, official guidance will tend to lead analysts to overstate the relative cost-effectiveness of civilians and understate the relative cost-effectiveness of military personnel.

Continue to Use Contractors to Augment and Extend the Civilian and Military Workforce

Our interviewees also indicated that contractors have unique advantages, especially the ability to provide surge capability, though NSA/CSS uses relatively few of them. Contactors enable IC managers to meet short-run requirements or requirements for highly specialized skills, such as less-used dialects. Our interviewees said that contractors also provide a "farm team" for the civilian workforce, and often are former military personnel who have recently left service. Contractors who are native speakers, however, may have difficultly getting cleared at the requisite levels and may have difficulties with English language proficiency. On the other hand, interviewees said that, because they focus only on their work with no collateral duties and their contracts can be terminated or extended relatively easier, contractors may have stronger performance incentives.

Improving the Management of Military and Civilian Language Professionals

While the focus of our analysis was on workforce mix, we were able to make some observations, informed by the people we interviewed and by the exploratory modeling analysis, about issues and possible recommendations for improving the management of military and civilian language professionals for the benefit of the defense and intelligence communities. Additional analysis would be required to assess the feasibility and effectiveness of these measures.

First, to ensure the career development of skilled language professionals, DoD and the military services might consider the possibility of creating a career path for military language professionals that deviates from the typical enlisted career. For example, some interviewees argued that DoD might consider making language professionals part of a warrant officer field, thereby allowing even mid-career and senior personnel to provide language capability in addition to being supervisors and leaders. Alternatively, like other "excepted communities," such as pilots, chaplains, and health professionals, language professionals might be in a separate competitive category of service, even for enlisted personnel. These alternative career paths might allow military language professionals to focus on developing and using language. They might enable community managers to promote personnel in part based on language capability and possibly reduce the collateral duties that currently divert the efforts of military language personnel away from providing language capability.

Second, DoD and the military services might consider recruiting military personnel who are already proficient or nearly proficient in a foreign language. Training military personnel who lack language proficiency takes time, and the model suggests that it puts them at a cost disadvantage relative to civilians. The modeling analysis suggests that recruiting military personnel who are proficient, or who require less extensive and time-consuming training, might reduce the relative cost of using military personnel. While additional analysis is needed about the most cost-effective and appropriate way to recruit language-proficient enlistees for specific missions, past research on recruiting policy suggests that offering incentives, such as bonuses and educational benefits, might be a promising approach.

Third, as part of the assessment of the costs involved in using one type of language professional over another, DoD should consider incorporating the net contribution of civilian language professionals who are former military personnel into the accounting of costs and benefits, and consider the feasibility and effectiveness of taking steps to encourage a greater flow of trained veterans with language capability into civil service jobs requiring language. Currently, veterans are given preference in civilian hiring, but civilian managers of functions for which military knowledge is important might consider offering higher recruitment bonuses to veterans with language skills. Furthermore, career counseling for military language personnel who are separating could explicitly provide guidance on language professional jobs in the IC.

Finally, policymakers might reconsider the constraints on the hiring of civilians, such as the authorization and appropriations processes, so that workforce managers can optimize the mix of personnel, including the hiring and employment of civilians into the government and military workforce.

Acknowledgments

We are deeply indebted to the language professionals and managers who met with us and participated in the interviews we conducted, especially at the National Security Agency/Central Security Service. Without their candid input, we could not have conducted this research. We are grateful to Alex Manganaris of the Office of the Director of National Intelligence who was the project monitor. We also would like to thank Carolyn Chu and Michael Lynch, former RAND employees, for their earlier work on the project and Kathi Webb and John Parachini at RAND for their input and guidance. We also appreciate the helpful input we received from the two internal RAND reviewers, Harry Thie and Bernard Rostker.

Abbreviations

CAPE	Cost Assessment and Performance Evaluation
DLIFLC	Defense Language Institute Foreign Language Center
DLPT	Defense Language Proficiency Test
DMDC	Defense Manpower Data Center
DoD	U.S. Department of Defense
DoDI	Department of Defense Instruction
DTM	Directive-Type Memorandum
FAR	Federal Acquisition Regulation
FY	fiscal year
GAO	U.S. Government Accountability Office
GS	General Schedule
IC	Intelligence Community
MEO	most efficient organization
NCS	National Cryptologic School
NSA/CSS	National Security Agency/Central Security Service
ODNI	Office of the Director of National Intelligence
OMB	Office of Management and Budget
OSD	Office of the Secretary of Defense
YOS	year of service

CHAPTER ONE

Introduction

Language professionals play a pivotal role in U.S. national security. The adversaries of the United States communicate their plans and actions in many different languages and dialects. Consequently, U.S. intelligence operations require personnel with high-level capability in these languages and dialects. Intelligence language professionals, be they military, government civilian, or contractor personnel, provide these vital skills. For example, in the area of signal intelligence, these professionals are required to listen to communications, decipher written and oral transmissions, and use and understand the colloquial phrases and syntax that are commonly used by native speakers of a language.

Given their pivotal role, policymakers want to ensure that language capability in the intelligence community (IC) is managed well. Among the issues involved in the management of this capability is the issue of what constitutes the best mix of personnel from among military, government civilian, and/or contractor personnel to provide this language capability to each IC mission. Each type of personnel provides different types of capability that contribute to IC missions, may result in different costs to the government, and may be constrained in their use by different factors to a varying degree. RAND was asked by the Chief Human Capital Office in the Office of the Director of National Intelligence (ODNI) to provide information to guide decisionmakers in their choice of workforce mix to provide language capability. This report presents the analysis and findings of this study.

To provide the requested analysis, we (1) identified existing policies and laws for determining personnel mix, (2) developed a framework that identified the factors that drive the cost and benefit of different personnel types, and (3) gathered information on those factors, obtained by quantitative and qualitative methods, as appropriate. To make our analysis more manageable, much of our analysis focused on one agency as a case study: the National Security Agency/Central Security Service (NSA/CSS).

We sought out the laws and policies that guide the choice of workforce mix within the U.S. Department of Defense (DoD) in part because NSA/CSS is an organization within DoD and in part because DoD guidance could be a prototype for similar guidance within ODNI, which currently does not have such guidance. DoD guidance provides considerable information on factors to consider in assessing the cost and benefits of different workforce mixes. We also drew from the economics literature, the defense manpower literature, and a recent DoD directive. The insights from the literature, together with the DoD guidance and policy on determining workforce mix, provide a framework for understanding the factors that affect the best mix of personnel in the IC. We then use this framework to inform a set of interviews we conducted on these factors with language personnel in the IC. We conducted interviews with language managers and with managers of functions that use language at DoD, ODNI, and NSA/CSS, as well as with language professionals themselves in NSA/CSS. This qualitative analysis is especially informative about factors for which there are no data or for which measurement is problematic. We supplemented the information from the interviews with an exploratory analysis of the cost and effectiveness of military versus government civilian language professionals. The analysis is exploratory because we were unable to gain access to NSA/CSS data on these personnel. Instead, we use multiple sources of information on the cost of military and civilian personnel to estimate costs and language proficiency. It is also exploratory because it is not a complete cost analysis; it focuses on the direct labor costs of military versus civilian personnel, ignoring contractors as well as other cost elements, such as overhead costs, material costs, and so forth. We conducted sensitivity analyses to assess to what extent our results might differ if we used data specific to the language community or made alternative assumptions.

Because the data analysis is not specific to the IC or to NSA/CSS language professionals, and the NSA/CSS case study focuses on one specific institution, our results should not be considered a definitive analysis of the best mix of language personnel at NSA/CSS or for specific missions in the IC. Rather, it provides information to guide further discussion about the best mix from a government-wide perspective. On the other hand, many of the issues and factors we consider have broader applicability to communities other than language professionals or NSA/CSS.

The report is organized as follows. Chapter Two briefly summarizes DoD guidance on determining the mix of military, civilian, and contractor personnel. Chapter Three summarizes our review of the literature, issues related to measurement of cost and effectiveness, and the factors that drive the cost and effectiveness of different sources of personnel. Chapter Four summarizes what we learned from the interviews, and Chapter Five summarizes the results from the exploratory model. We provide closing thoughts in Chapter Six. We provide several technical appendixes to describe our approach in more detail.

CHAPTER TWO

DoD Guidance for Determining Workforce Mix

DoD Instruction (DoDI) 1100.22, *Guidance for Determining Workforce Mix*, provides defense organizations with a framework for determining the mix of contractors, civilian, and military personnel to perform defense functions. The framework recognizes mission success, cost, and risk mitigation as important factors in determining the best source of personnel to perform an activity. ODNI does not have similar guidance for intelligence agencies. Because the framework in DoDI 1100.22 is written in a way that is generalizable to a broad array of functions, it can serve as an information source on factors that are likely to be important in the IC. Furthermore, this instruction could be a starting point for ODNI if it chooses to develop a workforce mix framework. While not explicitly stated, the guidance is based on a broad statement of benefits and costs, including the risks of performance by different sources of personnel—contractor, civilian, military—and it identifies the restrictions, exemptions, and exceptions that should guide the selection of each source.

This chapter presents an overview of the DoD guidance on workforce mix. More detailed information can be found in Appendix A and in Riposo et al. (2011). In this chapter, we do not discuss the implementation of the guidance. As discussed by Rostker (2008), implementation does not always accord with policy.[1] That said, our interviews did reveal some information about implementation at NSA/CSS.

The chapter begins by considering the restrictions and exemptions on the use of contractors and the circumstances when government employees—whether civilian or military—are preferred. If these restrictions or exemptions do not apply, DoD guidance instructs defense organizations to designate government civilians as the preferred source of personnel, unless there is an exception that argues for the use of military personnel. The chapter then describes these exceptions.

The criteria and guidance we discuss are inputs to the interview protocol we used in our interviews of key stakeholders. The interview protocol is presented in Appendix B, and the discussion of the interview results are presented in Chapter Five.

---

[1] For example, Rostker discusses how federal government agencies are able to employ contractor services without undergoing the formal competition process, known as the A-76 process (in reference to Office of Management and Budget (OMB) Circular A-76, the policy document that guides competitions between private and public sourcing of government functions).

Overview of Department of Defense Criteria and Guidance

DoD policy is that the DoD workforce should be established to "execute defense missions at a low to moderate level of risk" and that "risk mitigation should take precedence over cost-savings when necessary to maintain appropriate control of government operations and missions." While contractors may perform an activity at less cost, DoD guidance restricts the use of contractors if the risk or cost to the nation would outweigh any efficiency gain. DoD places three major restrictions on the use of contractors in defense organizations, as described by Riposo et al. (2011):

- inherently governmental functions
- functions closely associated with inherently governmental functions
- personal services.

Inherently governmental is defined by the government in different sources, but the general idea is the same: *Inherently governmental functions* refers to activities that are "intimately related to the public interest." These include activities that require the exercise of substantial discretion when applying government authority or value judgments when making decisions for the government. Inherently governmental functions can encompass a wide range of activities but certainly include the direction and control of crisis situations on behalf of the government and signing agreements on behalf of the government or otherwise binding U.S. interests. They may also be activities that would present contractors with a conflict of interest. In short, the basis for this restriction is that contractor performance of inherently governmental functions would result in a substantial risk to U.S. government concerns; therefore, it is mandated that inherently governmental functions be performed only by government employees.

Functions closely associated with inherently governmental functions are those that could otherwise be outsourced to a contractor, but the way they are performed or the circumstances under which they are performed result in higher risk and so may prevent contractor performance or make contractor performance only preferable under special circumstances. The Federal Acquisition Regulation (FAR) provides a list of examples, including activities that would allow contractors to gain access to confidential business information or activities where it might be assumed that contractors are agency employees or representatives. Like inherently governmental functions, functions closely associated with inherently governmental functions are those whose cost in terms of the risk to the nation is too great for them to be performed by a contractor.

Contractors are also prohibited from providing *personal services*. The FAR, subpart 37.104, defines personal services as those that create an employer-employee relationship between the government and the contractor employee. That is, the contractor appears as a government employee. In a personal services relationship, the government has continuous control and provides continuous supervision of the contractor. Some of the issues to consider in determining whether a contract is considered a personal services contract include whether the service is performed on-site with government furnished equipment, is also performed by military and civilian employees, requires government supervision, and is expected to last longer than one year.

If these three restrictions do not apply, then an activity or function is considered a commercial activity and could potentially be performed by a contractor. The exception is commercial activities that are exempted from private-sector performance because of law, executive order, treaty, or international agreement. Furthermore, DoD exempts activities from contractor performance as needed and designates them for military or DoD civilian employee performance if they provide for the readiness and workforce management needs of DoD. Specifically, the following factors may lead to an exemption from contractor eligibility:

- DoD readiness needs
  - operational risk
  - continuity of operations
  - dual tasking for wartime assignments
- workforce management needs
  - esprit de corps
  - overseas, sea-to-shore, and civilian/military rotation needs
  - civilian and military career development
  - DoD management decision.

Each of these types of exemptions is discussed in detail in Appendix A. In short, *operational risk* refers to situations where contractor performance would result in an unacceptable risk, such as critical combat operations or other essential functions during a crisis. *Continuity of operations* refers to the need to ensure that a critical "mass" of people are available to continue to perform government functions during a national emergency or wartime or to perform government functions in peacetime when personnel transfer in and out of activities. *Dual tasking wartime assignments* refers to assignments that meet DoD's need for an adequate pool of personnel performing commercial activities in peacetime who could fill critical assignments or serve as replacements for personnel assigned to the operating forces during a mobilization, crisis, or war. Activities that support *esprit de corps* are ones that help maintain military recruiting and retention by fostering public support for DoD. Assignments and activities that support the *rotation base* are ones that help maintain oversea tour lengths and sea-duty lengths at appropriate levels by providing assignments within the U.S. or on-shore. Those that support *career development* are ones that help ensure reasonable opportunities for DoD personnel to develop their careers and progress through the ranks. Finally, *DoD management decision* refers to decisions that exempt an activity from contractor performance, such as when it is under review and pending a decision.

If an activity or function is not exempt, DoD guidance is to designate the function as civilian, except when one or more of the following is true: There are reasons to designate it as military, an approved analysis shows that DoD civilians are not the lowest-cost provider of the function, or there is a legal, regulatory, or procedural impediment to using civilians.

The reasons to designate a function as military include the following:

- Military-unique knowledge and skills are required.
- Military incumbency is required by law, treaty, or international agreement.
- Military performance is needed for command and control, risk mitigation, or esprit de corps.
- Military manpower is needed to provide for overseas and sea-to-shore rotation, career development, or wartime assignment.
- Unusual working conditions or costs make the function not conducive to civilian employment.

If none of these circumstances are relevant, then DoD policy is to use civilians to perform a function, unless a cost analysis indicates that they are not the lowest-cost provider (or if there are other impediments to using civilians). Circular A-76 provides government agencies with guidance on how to conduct both a standard and a streamlined competition to determine the lowest-cost provider of a commercial activity.

Circular A-76 first calls for a public announcement of the competition. The procedures in the guideline differ somewhat for a standard versus a streamlined competition but generally include the same types of tasks. If the agency conducting the competition performs the function, the agency develops a cost estimate of the most efficient organization (MEO). The MEO is the proposed staffing plan that the agency would use to conduct the work that is to be done, i.e., how it would meet the workload, the performance standards, and the quality-assurance surveillance plan. A selection board then evaluates the agency's tender and the private sector offers, based on such criteria as the technical approach, personnel qualifications, and understanding of the requirements, and makes a decision about which offer to choose. The performance decision can be based either on which source is the lowest-cost provider or on factors other than cost. That is, the selection board can trade off factors other than cost in the selection process when doing so is in the best interest of the government and the perceived benefit is documented. Thus, according to the guidance, the agency must consider the best value in selecting proposals in terms of which source of personnel—contractor or government—can provide the greatest benefit in terms of performance of the desired work at the least cost.

CHAPTER THREE

Literature Review on the Costs and Benefits of Different Categories of Personnel

DoD guidance is that risk mitigation takes precedence over cost-savings in choosing different personnel categories, and civilian manpower is the preferred source of personnel unless a cost analysis shows that this source is not the lowest-cost source. This chapter presents information relevant for conducting such a cost analysis. We draw on information in the economics literature, past defense manpower studies, and recent guidance from the Office of the Secretary of Defense, Cost Assessment and Performance Evaluation (CAPE). We use the CAPE guidance because it is the current guidance on determining manpower mix in DoD. Other guidance is available, such as the cost estimating and assessment guidelines provided by the U.S. Government Accountability Office (GAO, 2009), but that guidance is quite general and not specifically focused on manpower mix issues. Dahlman (2007) considers the cost of a military person-year, focusing on how changing the method for computing the expected retirement liability of military personnel from that used by the DoD Office of the Actuary can result in different cost estimates and manpower mix decisions. There have been some critiques of the CAPE guidance, and we discuss these later in the chapter.

We incorporated the information in this chapter into the interview protocol and the exploratory cost analysis, and used the information to better understand the responses we get from the interviews. The discussion begins by first considering how to measure cost and benefit, both in terms of resolving some broad issues in cost and benefit measurement as well as in terms of assessing specific cost elements. It then considers the typical major drivers of the cost and benefit of different categories of personnel and why they are relevant.

Broad Issues to Consider When Measuring Costs and Benefits

There are four broad questions that should be addressed when measuring the costs and the benefits of different categories of personnel (Palmer et al., 1992; Robbert, Williams, and Cook, 1999; Gotz et al., 1990):

- Cost or benefit to whom?
- Cost or benefit over what time horizon?
- Cost or benefit of what?
- Average cost or the change in cost?

Cost or Benefit to Whom?

Because agencies are concerned about their own budgets, they will tend to focus on their own costs and benefits and ignore any spillover or intergovernmental transfers across agencies. However, from the standpoint of efficiency and maximizing the effectiveness of taxpayer resources, the relevant concept is the cost or benefit to the taxpayer. This issue is particularly relevant in the IC, where agencies may use both military and civilian personnel. A given workforce mix decision might reduce personnel costs for the agency of interest, but have an indirect spillover effect that increases military personnel costs to DoD. Because the agency does not account for the spillover effect on DoD, it may choose a workforce mix that results in an overall higher cost to the taxpayer while reducing the cost borne by that agency. For this reason, the research sponsor in ODNI requested that we consider the relevant costs and benefits to the government as a whole, and therefore the taxpayer, rather than to one specific agency or functional area.

That said, given that agencies will tend to take an agency-specific perspective in making cost-effectiveness comparisons, implementing a government-wide perspective in costing analysis would be nontrivial and require a change in the policy and guidance that agencies follow. For example, a possible (radical) implementation strategy for taking a government-wide perspective in manpower decisions in the IC is to make ODNI the sole resource provider of the entire IC workforce, not unlike a military service that funds personnel centrally and then allocates manpower to organizations within the service. Questions of implementation are important and could be a useful area for decisionmakers to consider, but such questions are beyond the scope of this report. Beyond implementation, the assessment of the costs and benefits of different workforces could differ from an agency perspective versus from a government-wide perspective. Thus, it is important to recognize that our results are applicable at the government, but not necessarily at the agency, level.

Cost or Benefit Over What Time Horizon?

Regarding the second question, the time horizon over which costs and benefits are computed is important because a focus on the short term will potentially ignore important future costs or benefits. Specifically, the time horizon should be long enough to incorporate the career patterns of personnel, because careers can differ significantly across different personnel types. For example, military personnel have shorter careers on average than government civilians, but military personnel have some chance of transitioning to the civilian or contractor workforce upon separation from the military. Consequently, a given number of military personnel may provide work years, and hence contribute to performance in the IC, well beyond those years provided while serving in uniform. Thus, the contribution of military personnel to mission readiness or accomplishment must incorporate their civilian career contributions. On the other hand, because civilians have longer careers and are more experienced, fewer civilians would be required to achieve a given level of readiness or performance, fewer civilian accessions will be needed to sustain a civilian force of a given size, and training and accession costs are amortized over more work years.

Similarly, career-related costs may differ by personnel type. Retirement costs for military and civilian personnel are realized in the future as a result of using personnel today. The DoD Office of the Actuary computes an actuarial cost of the active military retirement benefit that is allocated across the active force so that, over a typical career, sufficient funds are placed in the military retirement fund to cover expected retirement costs.[1] The Office of Personnel Management actuary makes a similar actuarial calculation of the cost of the civil service retirement programs.

Cost or Benefit of What?

Regarding the third question, assessments of the best workforce mix should focus on computing the costs and benefits of achieving a desired level of mission performance or accomplishment using different types of personnel. Because of performance or cost differences across type, the cost or benefit of achieving a desired state of readiness or mission accomplishment may require different numbers of personnel of each type. For example, if the average civilian employee provides greater language capability than an average military member, or stays in service longer, then fewer civilians are needed than military personnel to achieve a given mission objective.

Average Cost or the Change in Cost?

Regarding the fourth question, assessments of workforce mix should focus on the incremental costs or benefits of meeting a desired level of mission readiness or accomplishment with different personnel types rather than the total or average costs or benefits. The reason is that some costs and benefits, such as base operating costs, are common to all types of personnel, so these costs and benefits do not affect the change in cost among different mixes of personnel. Similarly, some factors affecting readiness, such as overhead costs or the operational environment, are fixed and do not depend on the type of personnel used, and these costs and benefits should be excluded as well. Thus, the scope of the analysis should be on the relative cost and benefits of personnel rather than the absolute levels.

Though the analysis should not include fixed factors that do not change as personnel types change, the analysis should incorporate changes in overhead costs or factors that affect benefits if they change as a result of the change in the mix of personnel. For example, to the extent that changes in the personnel mix involve major changes in infrastructure and technology, then the analysis should include the changes in these investments.

Specific Cost Elements

DoD Directive-Type Memorandum (DTM) 09-007 provides information on the cost elements and methodology for estimating and comparing the full cost to the government of DoD manpower (i.e., military and government civilian manpower), and of contractor services to make workforce mix decisions. We use this information in estimating cost of military and civilian personnel in our cost-effectiveness modeling in Chapter Five.

There are two groups of cost elements to consider for DoD manpower (i.e., military and government civilian personnel): direct costs and indirect costs. Direct costs are payments made for resources and assets that are used by the function under consideration. Indirect costs are payments made for resources and assets that support the function but are not directly attribut-

---

[1]   Past studies have criticized the DoD actuarial methodology for evaluating the cost of a military work year, and demonstrated alternative, more accurate, approaches to incorporating retirement costs into the cost of a military work year (Dahlman, 2007).

able to the function under consideration. Within each of these categories, direct versus indirect, are different factors.

Direct costs can be further divided into labor versus non-labor costs and within the labor category. Direct non-labor costs are costs that are not labor-related but are driven by the number of personnel in a workforce; for example, office space. Direct labor costs include those that are paid for by DoD and those incurred by other federal agencies. Because the focus of our analysis is on the cost to the taxpayer, we include both costs to DoD and to other agencies, including the Treasury. Table 3.1, copied from Table 1 in DTM 09-007, lists the elements of direct labor costs for military and civilian personnel.

Each row in the table corresponds to a type of direct labor cost: short-run variable costs, short-run fixed costs, and deferred pay-as-you-go costs. Short-run variable costs are those that

Table 3.1
Direct Labor Cost Elements for Military and DoD Civilian Personnel

| Cost | Military | | Civilian | |
	DoD	Other Federal Agency	DoD	Other Federal Agency
Variable costs in the short run	Basic pay Allowances and special pays Health benefit, active duty and dependents Social Security and Medicare Retired pay (accrual) Travel (PCS) transportation subsidy Education assistance Health benefit retiree (>65 MERHCF accrual) Training costs (amortized over years of practice) Recruitment, advertising, etc. (amortized)	Concurrent receipt (Treasury) Military Retirement (Treasury) MERHCF (Treasury) Child education (Education)	Basic pay/locality pay Allowances and special pays Incentive/Performance awards Health benefit (government share of FEHBP) Social Security and Medicare Retired pay (government share) Travel/PCS/ transportation subsidy/ relocation bonus Education assistance Overtime/holiday/other pays Life insurance/worker's compensation benefits Recruiting, advertising, etc. (amortized)	
Fixed costs in short run	Child development Family support services Discount groceries		Child development	
Deferred pay-as-you-go costs	Health benefit, retiree (<65 retiree and family) Health benefit, other (TAMP and CHCBP) Discount groceries, retiree Separation pay and travel Unemployment benefits Death gratuities Survivor benefits	VA benefits (Veterans Affairs) Employment training (Labor)	Severance health benefit Severance pay/incentive	Retirement benefit (CSRS unfunded) Health benefit Life insurance benefit

SOURCE: Directive-Type Memorandum 09-007, Table 1 (Department of Defense, 2010).
NOTES: PCS = Permanent Change of Station; MERHCF = Medicare-Eligible Retiree Health Care Fund; FEHBP = Federal Employees Health Benefits Program; FEHBP = Federal Employees Health Benefits Program; CSRS = Civil Service Retirement System; TAMP = Transitional Assistance Management Program; CHCBP = Continued Health Care Benefit Program.

are directly related to and are driven by the number of people in a workforce, such as basic pay. Short-run fixed costs are costs associated with services or goods that are not directly related to workforce size but may be adjusted over time if the size of the change in the workforce and the time horizon is long enough to justify a change, such as day-care centers and commissaries. Deferred pay-as-you-go costs are costs incurred in the future that are associated with workforce decisions made today. For example, health benefits for military retirees who are not eligible for Medicare is a pay-as-you-go cost; the liability incurred today of using personnel is paid for later when those personnel retire and become eligible for those health benefits.

Turning to indirect costs, these are cost elements that are not directly associated with the function under consideration but that could change as a result of workforce size or mix decisions. Often, these are the cost of support activities, such as overhead costs, or the fair share of support costs if those activities also support other functions not under consideration. For example, legal services; accounting; human resources; and cleaning, maintenance, and facilities-related services could all be considered indirect cost elements. Because indirect costs are unlikely to change much with workforce mix decisions, we ignore them in our exploratory analysis in Chapter Five.

In addition to direct and indirect costs, there may be miscellaneous other costs that are affected by workforce size and mix and that should be incorporated into a cost analysis. DTM 09-007 discusses the need to include implementation and transition costs that are not common to both alternative workforces under consideration. For example, the cost of relocating civilian employees as a result of a workforce mix decision would be a miscellaneous implementation cost.

DTM 09-007 also discusses the cost elements of a contractor workforce. Because NSA/CSS does not use a large contractor language workforce, relative to the overall language workforce, we ignore this group in our analysis of cost-effectiveness in Chapter Five. For completeness, and because other IC organizations use contractors, we mention here some of the key cost elements associated with contractors.

The full cost of a service contract is the negotiated price of the contract plus additional indirect costs. According to the guidance, the contract price, in turn, should include direct costs (labor and non-labor) as well as indirect costs borne by the contract, such as overhead costs, plus an allowance for profit. The full cost should also include additional indirect costs that arise as a result of using a service contract. For example, it should include the (fair share of the) cost of goods and services provided in-kind to the contractor and the cost of services performed by DoD to support the contract, such as administration and oversight activities.

Finally, DTM 09-007 provides guidance on computing the cost of manpower conversions (e.g., military to civilian or vice versa) versus the cost of a DoD manpower workforce relative to a service contract. The cost of a conversion (such as military to civilian) should include all direct and indirect labor costs that are not common to both categories of personnel, assuming the workforce size stays constant. If the size varies, then adjustments must be made to account for the difference. The guidance states that cost comparisons between DoD manpower and the contractor must account for whether the activity is performed off-site or on a government site. If performed on-site, then the guidance says that common costs for equivalent numbers of government and contractor personnel can be excluded. If performed off-site, the full cost of a service contract must include additional expenses the government incurs when a service contract is used rather than when the activity is performed by government workers.

Berteau et al. (2011) critique the DoD guidance and provide a list of its shortcomings. Their main criticism is that the guidance focuses on the cost to DoD and leaves out costs and savings that could accrue to other federal agencies. Other shortcomings raised by the study include issues related to the treatment of foregone tax receipts to the Treasury or state and local governments, the exclusion of the cost of DoD-owned capital for government workforces but not contractors, and the failure to account for the risk of cost growth and for varying work-load stability. Berteau et al. argue that OMB Circular A-76, the cost comparison methodology used by DoD prior to DTM 09-700, provided a better basis for performing cost comparisons but also has some flaws. The provides their own cost estimation methodology to address these flaws and shortcomings.

Chapter Five presents our exploratory cost analysis. The analysis focuses on direct labor cost elements, including those listed in the DTM and Table 3.1. The direct labor cost we use is the cost to the government, regardless of which agency pays the cost (DoD or NSA/CSS). Because the analysis is exploratory and does not include other cost elements, such as overhead costs, material costs, and capital costs, Berteau et al.'s (2011) criticisms related to those issues are not relevant to the cost analysis in Chapter Five.

Factors That Drive Cost and Benefit of Different Personnel Categories

We also sought information from the available literature on the drivers of the cost and benefits of different personnel categories and the reasons behind them. In this subsection, we review the broad literature on the major conceptual factors affecting cost-effectiveness and why they are relevant. We investigate whether these factors are important for language capability in the IC in later chapters. We incorporate these factors in our interview protocol and exploratory analysis.

Differences in the costs and benefits of using different personnel may stem from differences in productivity, according to the labor economics literature. The term *productivity* refers to the array of ways that personnel contribute to readiness and effectiveness, which can include not just the amount of work performed but also other dimensions, including the quality of work, timeliness, and responsiveness. Some of the major factors identified by the literature that may affect productivity, and therefore drive cost and benefit, include knowledge, skills, and abilities; availability and flexibility; incentives; and miscellaneous factors.

Knowledge, Skills, and Abilities

One important factor affecting productivity, according to human capital theory, is the knowledge, skills, and abilities of personnel (Borjas, 2005). The cost of personnel is affected by knowledge, skills, and abilities; to attract and retain personnel who know more, are better skilled, and are more able, the government faces pressure to raise pay. According to the literature, differences in knowledge, skills, and ability reflect an array of underlying factors, such as training, education, heritage and ethnicity, and the amount and type of job experiences.

As shown in Appendix C, military and civilian personnel have significantly different expected years of experience overall, and this is particularly the case with signals intelligence skills. The armed forces are composed of mostly junior personnel, a reflection of the "youth and vigor" culture of the military, where most military careers are short; even for those who stay until retirement, the retirement system gives an incentive to retire after 20 years (Warner,

2006). On the other hand, military retirees typically have a second career in the civilian sector, including government service, before they retire completely from the labor force. In contrast, civilian personnel may spend their entire working career in the civil service, though possibly in different agencies or work centers, until they retire. While some civilian retirees may continue to work after they retire from the civil service, such employment does not usually constitute their major employment during their career.

In the case of language capability, the focus is naturally on knowledge, skills, and abilities with language. However, other capabilities may also affect the productivity of different categories of personnel (Borjas, 2005). These might include knowledge of the operational environment, knowledge of specific technologies or information systems, country or cultural expertise, or different analytical skills to analyze and report intelligence (in English). How knowledge, skills, and ability affect productivity may be influenced by other factors, such as technology, that, in turn, may vary with personnel category.

Military, civilian, and contractor personnel may have different knowledge, skills, and abilities. Current and former military personnel have capabilities that are specific to the military, such as knowledge of language specific to military operations. Government civilian personnel in the IC are generally more experienced and are four-year college graduates, and they may be more experienced supervisors and mentors. Contractors may be heritage speakers and have better familiarity with slang and colloquialisms. These examples are only some of the ways that military, contractor, and civilian personnel might differ in their knowledge, skills, and abilities; we seek to identify such differences as part of our qualitative and quantitative analysis.

Availability and Flexibility

Productivity may differ across personnel types because of differences in the availability and the flexibility of employing different personnel types. Availability and flexibility are the results of the policies and practices that affect time on the job and the ability to surge in the short term by requiring that personnel work longer hours or under more arduous conditions. These policies may include those related to the rotation of personnel in the military, deployments, overtime, and the degree to which personnel are required to participate in competing activities.

For example, rotation policies affect availability as well as productivity (Hix et al., 1998). The services rotate military personnel as part of their normal career paths. Rotation allows military personnel to gain a breadth of experiences but can be disruptive if it takes time for newly rotated personnel to be brought up to speed and learn job-specific skills.

Deployments can enhance individual skills and improve future productivity, but deployed personnel may have less time available to perform routine training or use other skills that improve productivity. All categories of personnel may be deployed, but different categories may experience differing amounts of deployment, and the negative effect of deployment on availability and flexibility may differ by category as well.

Similarly, activities such as physical training or administrative duties may serve to maintain and/or grow skills that contribute to overall future readiness. However, these activities can be unrelated to the member's current assignment, and so they may also reduce the availability of personnel during the day to complete current missions.

There may be administrative or cultural differences that lead to differences in the availability and flexibility in the use of different categories of personnel. For example, military members are generally considered to be on-call 24 hours a day, every day, including holidays and weekends. The "rapid response" culture of the military means that members recognize being on-call as a normal part of their military service. In contrast, civilians might expect to be paid overtime for working unusual hours. This administrative/cultural difference may not permit the flexible use of civilian personnel during off-hours.

Another potential reason for differences in the management flexibility associated with the use of different personnel types stems from limitations on federal hiring placed by Congress and the OMB. As described by Rostker (2008), these limitations mostly take the form of personnel ceilings on the number of federal employers that can make up an agency's headquarters. Thus, to hire a civilian, there must be a position and the agency must be within the ceiling. Furthermore, the hiring process in the federal civil service is notoriously long. In the case of contractors, there are no ceilings on contractor strength. If the agency can hire contractors without a competition, positions can be filled quickly, implying the potential for greater flexibility in the use of contractors over civilian employees.

Contractors may be less available to perform certain tasks that are inherently governmental. For example, according to DoD instruction, contractors are not permitted to perform quality control duties, supervision of governmental employees, and other governmental tasks. We explore whether these restrictions are important in practice in the language community in our interviews, as described in later chapters.

Incentives

Performance incentives can also affect productivity (Jensen and Meckling, 1976; Holmstrom and Milgrom, 1991, 1994; Alchian and Demsetz, 1972; Lazear and Gibbs, 2009), and to the extent that productivity differs, personnel costs differ as well. Contractor, government civilian, and military personnel are all managed under different compensation and personnel structures, so their incentives to perform differ.

The literature particularly focuses on contractor incentives and the role of incentive mechanisms and the terms of the contract in aligning contractor objectives with those of the entity letting the contract, i.e., the government. Contractors may have different incentives to perform than other categories of personnel to the extent that their contract can be terminated or not renewed relatively easily or that the incentive mechanism embedded in the contract closely ties compensation to their output. They may have stronger incentives to perform the tasks that are stipulated in their contract or that are rewarded. On the other hand, it may not be possible to stipulate in a contract every task to be performed in every possible circumstance, especially in situations where circumstances change frequently. Furthermore, there are formal procedures for selecting a contractor and terminating the contract, and the flexibility of using contractors will depend on the flexibility of these procedures.

Another issue frequently addressed in the literature pertaining to contractors is the problem of "hold-up" (Williamson, 1985; Klein, Crawford, and Alchian, 1978; Kogut and Zander, 1996; Poppo and Zenger, 1998). The theoretical literature hypothesizes that when the nature of work requires knowledge, skills, or other investments that are specific to the government or agency, contractors may have an incentive to threaten to "hold up" or stop work in order to get additional or higher payments. The theory states that, because the investment is specific, the government cannot easily hire a replacement, and, should the contractor stop work, the government may fail to realize a return on the specific investment it already made. The literature discusses how contracts may be written to mitigate this problem and identifies situations where it is less likely to be important. For example, the theoretical literature predicts that long-term ongoing contractual relationships are less likely to be subject to hold-up problems because a contractor in this situation has an incentive to maintain its reputation, to ensure continued employment in the future. Whether the hold-up problem is supported by the evidence and is relevant to the language community in the IC is an open question.

The literature also considers the incentives of civil service employees and military personnel. Much of the literature on incentives for government employees focuses on mitigating incentives for corruption, though a subset of studies consider incentives for enhanced productivity (Asch, 2005; Burgess and Ratto, 2003; Dixit, 2002). Unlike the literature on contractors, this literature does not consider how incentives for government workers affect workforce mix decisions.

Other Factors

Other factors may cause the benefits and costs of different categories of personnel to vary but are not easily categorized. One factor is differences in the "corporate culture" and "corporate history" that facilitates the workflow for different personnel types (Camerer and Vepsalainen, 1988; Lazear, 1995; Kreps, 1990) and can affect worker productivity and cost. In the case of the military, Carl Builder (1989) discusses the different "personalities" of each branch of service and different service cultures. The literature highlights how having a common "corporate" language, routines, procedures, knowledge, and culture among personnel can be important because they can generate efficiencies by improving the coordination of people and tasks. The efficiencies are greater when communication is imperative for the performance of the work. According to the theory, outsiders, such as contractors, are more likely to be "foreign" to the corporate culture, unless they have prior experience with the specific organization and/or worksite. As discussed in Chapter Four, our interviews revealed that many contractors at NSA/CSS are former military personnel and likely have more of an "insider" perspective. According to theory, the importance of common culture and knowledge may vary with the mission.

Another miscellaneous factor that might affect productivity and cost differences across personnel categories is differences in economies of scale or scope associated with using different personnel types. An economy of scale means that average costs decline as the size of operations increase. Economies of scale may occur if there are large initial investments or fixed costs that must be incurred to set up or maintain operations, such as a human resource system or a purchase of a building site. As the scale of operations increases, the investment is defrayed over a larger number of units (or linguists), so the average cost declines.

An economy of scope is a related concept. While economies of scale refer to declining average production costs associated with one product line, economies of scope refer to declining average costs associated with multiple product lines. Thus, if a significant investment is made that is common to all product lines—for example, the cost of establishing a marketing strategy or a building site—the cost of the investment is defrayed as the number of product lines increases.

In the case of language capability, some investments might be fixed in terms of achieving a desired level of mission or functional readiness or accomplishment, regardless of the number of language analysts hired, the language they have, or the missions they support; these fixed investments are a source of economies of scale or scope. Alternatively, there may be investments that change with scale or scope, but not in a linear fashion. These investments might include aspects of the hiring process or of assigning and training language analysts. The importance of economies of scale or scope depends on the size of fixed investments. It may be the case that providing language capability has relatively few fixed investments and most costs vary with the number of language analysts and their language.

One potential source of fixed costs may be related to language training. While training costs, including the cost of maintaining language skills, will vary with the number of students, some training costs may be fixed or vary nonlinearly with the number of students. For example, the cost of an instructor to teach a given language course might be the same, whether one student or ten students are enrolled in the course. Furthermore, maintaining the training infrastructure might be a relatively fixed cost. However, as the number of students increases beyond ten, more instructors might be needed to teach more courses, but the costs might not rise in direct proportion to the number of students, allowing some economies of scale and scope.

From a theoretical standpoint, it is also not always clear whether contractors or government employees can better take advantage of economics of scale or scope. Contractors who serve many clients may be able to take advantage of economics of scale. On the other hand, large operations at a specific site, or centralized operations across many sites, may allow the government to take advantage of economics of scale or scope when employing governmental employees. Empirical information about the relative importance of these factors is needed to draw conclusions about the role of economies of scale or scope.

Another factor driving personnel costs and benefits is related to the magnitude of the skill set required and the duration of the requirement. If the skill set is highly specialized—for example, a particular dialect of a difficult and infrequently used language—it may be less costly for a contractor to acquire and maintain this skill set, if the contractor serves multiple clients on an ongoing basis. In contrast, if the government's or a specific agency's need is relatively small, infrequent, or of a short duration, it may be too costly to acquire and maintain the skill set within the government or agency.

A final factor is one that is specific to using contractor personnel: the cost associated with writing effective contracts. These transaction or contracting costs are costs that are over and above the costs of production. Contracting costs include the costs of negotiating, measuring, and enforcing the terms of the contract. These costs are higher when the tasks to be performed are complex, subject to considerable uncertainty, or change frequently. Some tasks are so complex or are performed in such a dynamic and uncertain environment that it is simply not possible to contract them to the private sector because it is impossible to predict every eventuality and stipulate the appropriate action to take under each circumstance. Furthermore, some tasks cannot be contracted because of legal limits (e.g., they are inherently governmental) or because they cannot be enforced by an objective third party (such as a court of law).

Summary and Implications for Assessing Workforce Mix

We drew from the economics literature, past defense manpower studies, and a recent DoD directive and identified four broad issues that must be resolved in measuring the cost and benefit of different personnel categories, to specify the cost elements that must be considered in measuring the cost of using civilian and military personnel, and to understand the major factors that could cause costs and benefits to vary among different categories of personnel and why. Together with the DoD guidance reviewed in the previous chapter, this information provides a framework for assessing workforce mix. We use this framework to develop the interview protocol we use for assessing the workforce mix of language professionals in the IC, to better understand the issues raised during the interviews, and to develop our exploratory model of the relative cost-effectiveness of a military versus a civilian language professional workforce.

Specifically, the four broad questions help guide the model development. For the question of "Cost or benefit to whom?" our research sponsor guided us to focus the exploratory model on measuring the cost and benefit of different categories of personnel to the government at large, rather than to a specific agency. Regarding the question of "Cost or benefit over what time horizon?" the model computes cost at a point in time but accounts for lifecycle related costs and benefits. For example, the model accounts for different expected career lengths among military versus civilian personnel. In response to the question of "Cost or benefit of what?" the model computes the cost to the government of achieving a given level of workforce language proficiency. Finally, in response to the question of "Average cost or the change in cost?" the exploratory model computes the cost and benefit of changing the workforce mix from an entirely military workforce to one that is composed of civil service personnel.

During the interviews, we were attuned to the factors identified in the literature that can cause cost and benefits of different personnel categories. Furthermore, the interview protocol includes questions related to these factors, such as the knowledge, skills, and abilities of different categories of personnel and the factors that affect them, such as education, experience, and training. It also includes questions about complementary skills that different personnel categories may embody and includes questions pertaining to the availability of personnel, including competing duties that they may have; questions about the flexibility to use different sources of personnel; and as questions related to the miscellaneous factors that can drive cost and benefit. That said, not every factor was discussed in every interview, and while we used the interview protocol as a guide, we also delved into more detail on subjects considered important by the interviewees, so not every topic was discussed at each interview.

We discuss the results of our interviews in the next chapter and the results of the exploratory model in Chapter Five.

CHAPTER FOUR

Insights from Interviews

This chapter describes our qualitative results. The purpose of this analysis was to obtain qualitative information on the factors that may affect language workforce mix decisions in the IC but that are not amenable to measurement or for which there is little data. Chapter Five presents the quantitative analysis.

The chapter begins with an overview of the methodology used, with a more detailed description given in Appendix B. It then summarizes the major themes that emerged from the interviews we conducted, beginning with a description of the general nature of work performed by language professionals at NSA/CSS. While the specific jobs may differ across missions and locations, we highlight some general characteristics of the work performed. Next, we discuss the limited role of contractors in providing language capability at NSA/CSS, so our focus is on military versus civilian personnel. We then describe what we learned about the perceived advantages and benefits as well as the perceived costs, limitations, and obstacles of using military personnel, and of using civilian personnel in the missions and locations we considered.

Overview of Approach

Because of the tremendous diversity of missions and capabilities that language professionals provide throughout the IC, we decided to focus the analysis on one specific agency, the NSA/CSS. Broadly speaking, a clear advantage of considering the NSA/CSS is that it employs a large number of language professionals, both military and government civilian, in a broad array of missions in multiple locations.[1] That said, there are disadvantages as well. The NSA/CSS employs relatively few contractors to provide language capability, and it is unclear how relevant information garnered from the NSA/CSS is to other agencies and areas of the IC. Furthermore, our interviews, the basis of our qualitative analysis, did not extend to every mission conducted by language professionals at NSA/CSS, or at every site. And our interviews were not with randomly selected groups. Thus, the information garnered from the interviews must be considered suggestive and not definitive. Nonetheless, they provide useful insights about the nature of the work performed by linguists in general, the contributions of different sources of linguists, and some challenges and problems faced by the NSA/CSS from different sources.

With the assistance of the NSA/CSS's senior language authority, we conducted numerous interviews within DoD, ODNI, and NSA/CSS. Both the interview protocol and the qualita-

---

[1]   Because we did not have access to workforce data in the IC, including the NSA/CSS, we are unable to provide statistics on the relative number of each category of personnel at NSA/CSS or other IC organizations. The statements here are based on input we received from the sponsor and from the interviews.

tive research approach were reviewed and approved by RAND's Institutional Review Board to ensure protection of human subjects. The interviews spanned a number of broad groups:

- Force provider managers: Managers within each service, within NSA, ODNI, and within the Office of the Secretary of Defense (OSD) who have oversight over the career management of language professionals and who administer personnel policies related to this community, including hiring, training, and compensation.
- Force users or product line managers within NSA: We interviewed managers of product lines within NSA/CSS that require language capability.
- Language professionals who supply language capability: We interviewed groups of employees, military and civilian, who provide language capability at the three NSA/CSS cryptologic centers.
- Language trainers: We interviewed managers and educators who provide language training at the Defense Language Institute Foreign Language Center (DLIFLC) and at the National Cryptologic School (NCS).

The interviews were conducted at the three cryptologic centers, as well as at NSA/CSS headquarters at Fort Meade. We also conducted interviews at DLIFLC in Monterrey, California, and interviews with force provider managers within DoD and ODNI in the Washington, D.C., area.

We used the interview protocol, provided in Appendix B, to guide the interviews. We did not seek responses to every question in every interview we conducted, so that we could explore themes raised by interviewees that they considered relevant to the topics we covered. The interview protocol was sent to interviewees ahead of time, so that individuals could have a chance to see the questions and prepare responses if they desired. Some interviewees provided written responses, and, where feasible, their responses are incorporated into our summary of findings. We prepared written notes from our interviews and compiled and organized them according to major themes. These themes are discussed next.

Major Themes Emerging from Our Interviews

We begin the discussion by describing the nature of the work performed by language professionals at NSA/CSS. This discussion draws from both the interviews and from open source material provided on the NSA/CSS website. We then discuss the major themes that emerged about the role of each category of personnel in providing language capability. We conclude with a summary and discussion of findings.

Nature of Work

DoD guidance for determining workforce composition applies criteria to jobs for assigning personnel from nongovernmental and governmental (military and civilian) sources. In determining the potential suitability of each category of personnel, the criteria focus on the activities to be performed for each job.

Our analysis focuses on jobs and activities performed at the National Security Agency that we were told require linguistic capability. The jobs and activities are performed in support of the overall mission of the NSA/CSS, "to protect U.S. national security systems and to produce foreign signals intelligence information . . . for intelligence and counterintelligence purposes and to support military operations" (NSA/CSS, 2009d).

Cryptology is at the core of the NSA/CSS's mission. Cryptology is a field of information security that entails protection of one's own sensitive communications, as well as the interception and deciphering of communications of one's adversaries (Webopedia, no date). The work of cryptology can involve the recording, transcribing, translating, analyzing, and reporting of communications through various modes (About.com—U.S. Military, no date).

Cryptological linguists support the cryptological function through the understanding of foreign languages. They may, for example, provide summaries, transcriptions, or translations of foreign communications as part of reports prepared by intelligence analysts (U.S. Army, no date).

While cryptological linguists provide key contributions to the NSA's missions, other jobs and functions also require language capability. Language analysis is a unique career field at NSA/CSS, offering various career paths that encompass analytical, supervisory, and teaching assignments (NSA/CSS, 2009b). The major duties include translation, transcription, research and reporting, and placing research and analysis in an appropriate cultural context (Makingthedifference.org, no date).

Knowledge of a designated language is critical to successful performance of these jobs and activities. Currently, NSA/CSS seeks expertise for "line" openings in Asian and Middle Eastern languages, including African, Dari, Farsi, Korean, Mandarin Chinese, Pashto, Urdu, and Punjabi (NSA/CSS, 2009b). Applicants for NSA/CSS positions require a Top Secret clearance (NSA/CSS, 2009c).

Our interviews revealed further insights into the nature of work requiring linguistic capability.

NSA/CSS work requires a high degree of language proficiency. The language professionals we heard from told us that it takes 5–8 years to become fully capable to perform most NSA/CSS language missions. This results from a combination of the need for a high degree of language proficiency and the development of so-called "target knowledge."

Many positions at the NSA/CSS requiring language proficiency are rated as requiring 3/3 (general professional proficiency) or higher. However, debate exists over whether all such positions actually require this level of proficiency, given the type of information being collected and analyzed, the experience and motivation of the employee, and the availability of support and supervisory resources to assist the employee. Nonetheless, it is generally understood that high levels of language proficiency are preferable.

NSA/CSS work may require deep "target knowledge." The NSA's mission is worldwide and encompasses a variety of topics that can relate to national security concerns. Information collected may be analyzed to provide strategic or tactical information; e.g., to war planners and warfighters. In addition, NSA/CSS provides products and services to a variety of U.S. government agencies and allies and coalition partners (NSA/CSS, 2009d). Depending on the field of interest, substantial expertise may be required in professional and technical disciplines, such as computer science, mathematics, or computer engineering (NSA/CSS, 2009a). Moreover, certain areas of interest may require a thorough understanding of history, culture, economics, and prior experience with respect to a particular foreign adversary. In addition, language capability is primarily measured in terms of Defense Language Proficiency Test (DLPT) scores, but the DLPT is not target- or mission-specific, so it may not capture the range of language capability required for some missions.

Our interviews suggest that the preponderance of missions requiring language capability at NSA/CSS are moving away from ones that emphasize traditional military issues involving particular adversaries (e.g., monitoring military movements) toward ones that focus on broader issues involving many more transglobal actors and languages (e.g., tracking proliferation of nuclear material). Additional emphasis is being placed on development of long-term strategic understanding of emerging trends (e.g., advances in industrial capability in particular countries), along with near-term tactical concerns. Furthermore, materials for analysis are no longer primarily formal communications, such as formatted publications, but now also include less formal modes of communication. Finally, certain missions (e.g., counterterrorism) are particularly demanding and complex in nature. Therefore, demand is growing for individuals with high levels of both substantive expertise and linguistic capability. This may alter the importance placed on different categories of personnel who provide language capability in performing these functions.

With these considerations in mind, we now move to a discussion of the attributes of various categories of personnel in the NSA/CSS workforce who possess language capability. We begin first with a discussion of the role of contractors.

Role of Contractors

A major fact, pointed out by our interviewees and readily observable in the settings in which cryptological work is performed at NSA/CSS, is that the vast preponderance of personnel performing these functions requiring language capability are government civilians or military personnel. Contractors are relatively few.

In this part of the IC, cryptological intelligence work is viewed as inherently governmental and thus "exempt" from private-sector performance. The work qualifies as inherently governmental according to numerous criteria; e.g., it requires discretion and decisionmaking authority, "direction and control" of military forces, and unique military knowledge and skills. We were told that the requirement for a Top Secret clearance for employment at the NSA/CSS further reinforces the perception that the work performed there falls within the governmental domain. Contractors can obtain Top Secret clearances, but given that such clearance is not necessarily a requirement for employment with a contractor, the perception is that individuals who work for contracting organizations may be precluded from working for NSA/CSS.

Utilization of contractors at NSA/CSS occurs not as a first choice but instead as a response when the supply of civilian and military personnel is insufficient. Contractors may be turned to as a source of "surge" capacity, when additional personnel are needed quickly to meet workload. Contract linguists do not need to be trained—they are hired already trained—and the time needed to get them into the workplace may be relatively short if a contract is already in place with a commercial provider. NSA/CSS may also turn to contractors when specialized skills are needed; e.g., for performing translations in a particularly rare language, slang, or dialect. Interviewees said that contractors may be hired and fired relatively quickly; hence, they can provide flexibility to respond quickly to short-term and changing requirements. Related to this flexibility is the sense among some functional managers we interviewed that contractors have a strong performance incentive because there are clear consequences to substandard performance. Our interviews did not cover any of the specific procedures or policies that are involved in hiring or firing contractors.

Moreover, contractors possess certain performance and cost characteristics that may cause them to be viewed unfavorably by government personnel. For example, they are precluded from doing certain types of functions (e.g., analysis and quality control of others' work). They cannot supervise military and government civilians. And it is commonly believed that other limitations, such as security clearance eligibility or English language proficiency among heritage speakers, may diminish their ability to contribute as effectively to the mission of the organization. That said, some of these limitations may yield other advantages. Some functional managers said in interviews that because contractors do not have collateral duties, they can focus more of their attention and effort on the language mission. As mentioned earlier, NSA/CSS employs relatively few contractors to provide language capability, so it is unclear how relevant information regarding contractors garnered from the NSA/CSS is to other agencies and areas of the IC

For these reasons, we focus primarily in the remaining discussion on the issues that distinguish military personnel and government civilians who provide language capability in the cryptological community.

Role of Military Personnel

According to DoD guidelines, once an activity is deemed "inherently governmental," criteria further specify whether functions and responsibilities may be assigned to government civilian versus military personnel. Generally, the "default" category is civilian, unless exceptions indicate that military personnel are preferable.

Our interviews affirm the existence of such "exceptions" in characterizing the contributions of military personnel providing language capability at the NSA. Examples of functions in which military members with linguistic capability may predominate include the following:

- missions that require deployment, especially to an austere military environment or within a combat zone
- missions that entail operational risk
- short-notice assignments away from home
- functions that draw on military-specific knowledge and skills
- missions that directly support war planners and warfighters.

Military personnel contribute broadly to cryptologic linguist and language analysis functions across the NSA. There are, however, a number of characteristics of military personnel that govern the nature of their contributions.

First-Term Enlisted Personnel Comprise the Majority of Military Staff at NSA/CSS

All military services are represented at NSA/CSS headquarters and at NSA/CSS field sites. Most of the military personnel are enlisted personnel, with junior enlisted predominating; relatively few are officers. For many enlisted personnel, NSA/CSS is their first assignment after graduating from the Defense Language Institute and advanced cryptological training. Therefore, these individuals may arrive at the NSA/CSS lacking previous military or deployment experience that could contribute to performance of certain missions. Relative to other, more experienced or better educated personnel, they may possess more limited "world knowledge" useful for analysis tasks requiring synthesis and interpretation. For example, some interviewees said that young people with only a high school diploma—like the typical junior enlisted member—have only limited world knowledge, which can be a limitation in cases where the mission or target requires understanding of culture, history, and common practices and requires intuition based on experience or exposure to different environments and customs. Lack of a college education may also mean that enlisted personnel have limited writing and analytic skills that are needed for some missions.

Furthermore, some interviewees stated that, because military personnel tend to be junior, they may require extensive supervision and mentoring to ensure successful performance. On the other hand, some interviewees stated that junior enlisted personnel who have completed training are obligated to complete their first enlistment contract, so managers can reliably count on military personnel to not attrite or leave NSA/CSS, at least until the end of their contract term or their rotation, whichever comes first.[2]

Military Personnel May Possess Insufficient Language Capability for Certain Missions

Earlier, we mentioned that many positions at NSA/CSS are rated 3/3 in required language capability. Military personnel assigned to NSA/CSS following graduation from the DLI may not meet these requirements; 2/2 is all that is required to qualify for graduation. Military personnel—junior and senior among them—assigned to DLIFLC after an operational assignment may or may not have maintained or enhanced their language skills, depending on the nature of the operational assignment. We were told that sometimes these personnel do not use their language skills while on an operational assignment, for a variety of reasons. For example, cryptologic linguists with a specific language (e.g., Korean) may be assigned to positions that require a different language (e.g., Arabic), so their language skills degrade. Also, some interviewees said that enlisted personnel are less adept with materials that are not formally formatted, use slang, and pertain to nontraditional missions. There is a perception among some of the interviewees that operational assignments often degrade language skills. Some stated that some military language professionals use their language skills regularly only while they are assigned at NSA/CSS but not when they have a military assignment, especially an operational one.

We also heard that, as military personnel become more senior, collateral duties and incentives for promotion diminish opportunities for maintaining and enhancing language capability, relative to opportunities to develop and enhance leadership and supervisory skills. Thus, while more senior military personnel at NSA/CSS may have better language skills, the job requirements of an E-6 or E-7 require that they supervise junior personnel who perform the language mission, rather than perform the language mission themselves. Consequently, some interviewees believed that NSA/CSS is not able to fully take advantage of the superior language skills of more senior military personnel who have the 5–8 years of service performing language that is deemed necessary to be fully mission capable. More generally, we heard from a number of interviewees that the military career path for language personnel does not optimize the use of language because, in general, those who have the least skill perform the language mission, while those who have the greatest skill do not.

An additional question that was raised in some interviews pertained to whether sufficient military personnel possess the "right" language skills. As indicated earlier, current requirements at NSA/CSS emphasize Asian and Middle Eastern languages. Military personnel are trained at DLIFLC in languages of importance to their respective services, which may reflect

---

[2]   We have no data on attrition rates of military linguists at NSA/CSS, so we were unable to verify how their attrition differs from that of military personnel overall. That said, our tabulations of separation rates for the analysis in Chapter Four show that average work years are lower for enlisted military cryptological linguists than for enlisted personnel overall, suggesting higher, not lower, attrition rates. See Appendix C.

different priorities than the NSA/CSS's. For example, there may be insufficient military personnel to meet requirements in some specific or scarce languages in demand at NSA/CSS (e.g., Punjabi). In addition, our interviews revealed that the DLPT focuses on testing "global" language skills rather than language skills required for specific missions or targets. NSA/CSS language professionals, including military personnel, receive training at the NCS, which, among other things, provides military personnel as well as others with target-specific language skills. However, some interviewees said that time spent in continuing education at the NCS was also time taken away from performing "on-target," i.e., performing a specific mission.

Some interviewees noted the uniqueness of DLIFLC in providing a steady flow of trained military language professionals en mass. There is no real civilian counterpart to DLIFLC in terms of scale and breadth. There is also no civilian equivalent of Goodfellow Air Force Base, where many military personnel receive training in cryptology.

Tour Lengths Limit the Contributions of Military Personnel

Assignments at the NSA/CSS typically occur for 2–3 years for military personnel. In general, military personnel rotate between operational field assignments in their service and headquarters assignments, which can include the NSA/CSS—though this pattern varies by military service. While follow-on NSA/CSS assignments can occur, assignments in general are driven by the needs of the military service, and continued service at the NSA/CSS cannot be assured. The comings and goings of military personnel limit their ability to develop language capability and deep target knowledge. Depending on the nature of the intervening assignments and opportunities to maintain language proficiency, their language capability may degrade and require remediation if they receive a repeat assignment to the NSA/CSS. On the other hand, frequent rotations enable military personnel to gain a breadth, if not depth, of experience that can prove useful in NSA/CSS missions.

Military Tours at the NSA/CSS Contribute to the Military Mission

We also heard from interviewees that a tour at NSA/CSS benefits military personnel and, more broadly, the military's ability to perform its missions. Interviewees said that working at NSA/CSS enables military personnel to gain a better understanding of the national mission relative to what they gain from a more tactical operational mission, to gain additional training at the National Cryptologic School, to improve their language skills through greater usage, and to develop a network of contacts of "who to call" or "who to ask" at NSA/CSS when they return to their operational tours. Finally, tours at NSA/CSS also support the rotation base for deployed service members. An NSA/CSS tour is "shore duty," so to speak, and enables members to gain training, address personal readiness issues (such as dental readiness), and be with their families and friends. Thus, an additional role of military personnel is to provide a positive feedback on the military mission.

Together, these characteristics of military personnel, coupled with changes in the nature of work that enhance the importance of language capability, create challenges for developing and utilizing military personnel as part of the workforce mix.

Management of Military Language Professionals Could Be Improved

We heard numerous suggestions and comments for improvements in managing the careers of military personnel to optimize language use and capability. We heard that their careers need to more strongly emphasize the use and development of language capability and deemphasize the development and use of leadership and other skills that lead to promotion. Specifically, interviewees suggested that military personnel need to explicitly focus on developing language skills throughout their careers, using language in every assignment rather than just assignments at NSA/CSS. Deployments can degrade language skills because those skills are often not used or maintained. Furthermore, personnel may be mismatched into assignments such that the required language skills in the assignment far exceed their capability, so they are unable to perform the mission effectively without additional investments in training or mentoring. Several interviewees suggested that military language professionals become warrant officers, so that their career development focuses on increased specialty proficiency, and even mid-career and senior personnel could provide language capability in addition to being supervisors and leaders. More generally, these interviewees suggested creating a career path for military language professionals that could deviate from the typical career profile for military personnel. In addition to the warrant officer idea, some interviewees suggested that language professionals, even enlisted personnel, be managed like a competitive category for service, such as is the case for pilots and chaplains, for example.

Role of Government Civilian Personnel

Government civilian personnel are found in a variety of jobs and functions requiring language capability at the NSA/CSS. Their roles can mirror those of military personnel and can compensate for some of their limitations. For example, while civilians may be less able to deploy to austere locations or take short-notice assignments, and may lack current military knowledge and experience, they possess additional attributes of value. According to our interviews, these can include the following:

- institutional knowledge and continuity
- deep technical expertise and/or deep target knowledge
- potentially, greater language capability and experience in using the language.

As with their military counterparts, however, interviews indicated that there are some additional key considerations that govern the nature of their contributions. These are discussed below.

Many Civilian Personnel Have Previous Military Experience

Previous experience is another key feature of the civilian workforce providing language capability at the NSA/CSS. NSA/CSS employees come from a variety of sources. Some are "fresh hires" from university language programs, while some transfer from other intelligence or defense agencies. Many of the latter, along with many new hires, are previously separated or retired military personnel who worked as cryptologic linguists in the military. Indeed, many received language training at the DLIFLC and held assignments at the NSA/CSS during their military career. Such prior military experience was considered particularly advantageous by some of the interviewees in missions and targets that required operational or military tactical knowledge. Because many civilian language professionals at NSA/CSS are prior-military personnel, especially those in assignments where such knowledge is valuable, some interviewees felt that military linguists were essential, if for no other reason than as a future source of civilian language professionals. In contrast, some interviewees said that those civilians who did not have previous military personnel were at a disadvantage for some operational missions because they had less familiarity and connection to the warfighter.

A related issue that was noted by some interviewees is the value of the military as a source of a large number of language professionals. Some argued that civilian sources of language capability provide only a "trickle" of personnel with the necessary security clearance. In their view, only the military, and specifically DLIFLC and subsequent cryptologic training such as at Goodfellow Air Force Base, provide large flows of language professionals to national security missions.

Civilian Personnel Are Typically Older and Have More Experience

In contrast to military personnel, civilians are typically older; have more experience, including experience at NSA/CSS; and typically have more education, such as a college degree, according to interviewees. This greater seniority and better education typically make civilians more productive at many missions and targets. Furthermore, mid-career and senior civilians continue to provide language capability, and their greater education and experience means they are likely to have not only greater language capability but also deeper target knowledge, a broader global perspective of culture and history relevant for some missions, and more extensive world knowledge and intuition based on exposure to different environments and customs. Some interviewees commented that while their greater job experience provided more depth in terms of target knowledge, civilians sometimes lack breadth of exposure to different missions and operational environments.

Nonetheless, government civilian personnel are often called upon for a variety of activities, including providing intelligence analysis summaries, report writing, and supervising and mentoring military personnel. Furthermore, because contractors are precluded from performing inherently governmental tasks, and their activities are dictated by the terms of their contracts, civilians are generally called upon to research, summarize, report, and perform a host of other miscellaneous activities. Some interviewees stated that these collateral activities detracted from their "time on target" and ability to provide language capability.

Hiring Constraints Limit the Availability of Government Civilians with Language Skills

The total number of available civilian positions at the NSA/CSS is established in congressional authorizations bills and may be further limited by appropriations provided by Congress for civilian salaries. Moreover, civilian positions are assigned to organizations within the NSA/CSS according to management priorities. Billets for civilian language and cryptologic analysts "compete" with billets for other civilian positions within overall limits; this may limit the availability of civilians with language skills in certain parts of the organization.

An additional constraint involves the hiring of government civilians at NSA/CSS field sites. These positions are also governed by allocation decisions made at headquarters and may result in a shortage of civilians with particular language skills at certain sites. That is, recruiting is centralized at the NSA/CSS headquarters level, and some interviewees at the field sites stated that they felt that centralization limited their flexibility to hire personnel locally that met their needs in a timely manner. Local hiring managers sometimes stated that additional flexibility in decisionmaking procedures could assist the hiring of civilians at local field sites. In addition, specific field sites may be unattractive to civilian employees with respect to geographic location, cost-of-living considerations, and so forth. For these reasons, the mix of military versus civilian personnel favors military personnel at the field sites relative to the headquarters.

Constraints on Personnel Management Affect Civilian Personnel

Our interviews identified constraints inherent in the government civilian workforce that can decrease management's flexibility in reassigning personnel and changing workforce composition to meet changing mission requirements. Rules governing personnel management can make it difficult to fill civilian positions in a timely manner or to discharge individuals with lack of cause, even if the language in which the individual is proficient is no longer in demand. Also, government employees' work hours are limited. Though many are fully dedicated and work extra hours on their own, budget may not exist to pay overtime; hence, supervisors may be reluctant to ask government civilians to work extra hours. Finally, government employees may not be moved arbitrarily across positions or forced to relocate.

Military personnel, on the other hand, can be redirected into different positions, sent away on short-notice assignments, and required to work extra hours as part of ordinary military regimen. For these reasons, they are often used to meet near-term needs and fill personnel gaps. Similarly, contractors in roles appropriate to them may be obtained quickly and can be discharged rapidly if their services are no longer needed. In a way, the constraints on the management of government civilian employees define the use of military personnel and contractors.

Summary

Our interviews provided a number of insights about the nature of work performed by language professionals, the contributions of different categories of language professionals to NSA/CSS, the contribution of NSA/CSS assignments of military personnel to the armed forces and their costs, the constraints on the use of different categories of personnel, and possible areas of improvement in their management.

Civilian personnel provide the "backbone" of the NSA/CSS workforce. On the whole, they offer the highest level of language proficiency and depth of target knowledge, particularly in topics requiring nonmilitary expertise, which are growing in importance. They play key roles as analysts and as supervisors. They potentially offer more continuity to the organization than any other category of personnel. For these reasons, a common sentiment expressed in our interviews was that "the NSA needs more civilians" providing language capability to NSA/CSS missions. This was particularly the case in some of the field sites.

Military personnel also bring unique advantages, particularly for those missions that require tactical military knowledge and understanding of the operational environment. They are unique in their ability to deploy and provide connectivity between military planners and warfighters and headquarters. While generally more junior and potentially somewhat less proficient at language, they contribute and can be successfully mentored and developed. Most importantly, perhaps, the military provides a mass quantity of linguists through the DLIFLC and serves as a "farm team" for subsequent civilian employment.

Contractors also bring unique advantages, particularly as they provide management flexibility in meeting changing skill requirements and supporting "surge" operations as temporary adjunct staff. Provided they can meet security requirements, they may also be viewed as a "farm team" for subsequent civilian employment. On the other hand, contractor support is limited to non–inherently governmental activities and those activities that can be and are stipulated in their contracts. Contractors do not receive training, so unless they have the requisite target-specific skills already, they are of limited use. Finally, contractors may be drawn from among the U.S. foreign national population. Insofar as getting a security clearance is difficult for individuals from specific countries of origin or with certain background experiences, contractor support may limited.

In conclusion, the interviews provide extensive information about factors driving workforce mix considerations that are not easily amenable to measurement. However, the interviews yielded little quantitative information on the cost or on the benefits of different categories of personnel. For this reason, we also conducted a quantitative analysis of the relative cost of providing language proficiency of different categories of personnel. The results of the analysis are presented in the next chapter.

CHAPTER FIVE

Exploratory Analysis of the Relative Cost-Effectiveness of Military Versus Civilian Language-Proficient Workforces

It is useful to supplement the interview findings with computations of the difference in the cost of providing language capability to the IC with different categories of personnel. Because of data limitations, we were not able to make such computations. Instead, we developed an exploratory model, so described because (1) we do not use information specifically for language personnel in the IC, (2) we focus on military and civilian personnel but not contactors, and (3) we consider only direct costs and not other cost categories. We exclude contractors because of a lack of data and information on these personnel.[1] Furthermore, the model embeds assumptions where data are missing. Nonetheless, it provides some initial insights into the cost-effectiveness of military versus government civilian language personnel in the IC from a government-wide perspective and can serve as a starting point for computing relative cost-effectiveness when IC-specific data are available; it also provides a "first look" at what the results of such an analysis might reveal. We also note that the findings about the relative cost-effectiveness of government civilian relative to military personnel are consistent with what we heard in the interviews, described in Chapter Four. Thus, this quantitative analysis is complementary and consistent with the qualitative analysis in terms of the broad factors affecting workforce mix decisions for establishing language capability.

The model we developed measures language capability as the number of work years provided by a given workforce type, adjusting for the amount of language proficiency that the workforce provides. To compare different workforces, we compute the difference in the cost of providing the same amount of "work" when that work is provided by a military versus a civilian workforce. Thus, the model provides rough estimates of the net cost per expected work year of a military versus civilian workforce providing the same amount of proficiency.

We recognize that, in reality, a workforce providing language proficiency in the IC is likely to include both military and civilian personnel, and even contractors. Thus, the comparison of a military workforce with a civilian one in this analysis is meant to illustrate the relative cost-effectiveness of one personnel type over another and not meant to provide cost estimates of a workforce of a specific mix.

More specifically, in considering the difference in cost of a military workforce, we recognize that the expected work years of enlisted members include not just their military career but also their expected work years after they leave the military and work as civilians providing language proficiency. Thus, for the analysis presented in this chapter, the term *military workforce* refers to both enlisted personnel and veteran civilian personnel. The comparison group is

---

[1] Gates (2009) discusses the need for better data on the contractor workforce for manpower mix decisions.

a civilian workforce consisting of only nonveterans.[2] As we explain in Appendix C, we compute the net cost or the difference in cost of the military workforce relative to the comparison nonveteran civilian workforce. Similarities in the contributions of each workforce are netted out. Consequently, our computation of relative cost-effectiveness considers only the marginal or additional contributions of veterans relative to nonveteran civilians. As discussed in Appendix C, veterans are assumed to enter the civil service at a higher level of proficiency, but their advantage is temporary.[3]

This chapter begins with an overview of the model, with more details provided in Appendix C. We then describe the cases we consider, specifically the base case and two sets of alternative case. Next, we describe the modeling results, and we conclude with a summary.

Model Overview

There are two major components of the computation of the difference in the cost per expected work year when proficiency is provided by the military workforce versus the civilian workforce: (1) an estimate of expected proficiency-adjusted work years and (2) a measure of cost for each workforce type. We must consider three groups: enlisted personnel while they are in the military; civilians who are former military personnel (veteran civilians), and civilians who are nonveterans (nonveteran civilians). The first two groups make up the military workforce, and the third group is the comparison nonveteran civilian workforce.

To compute proficiency-adjusted expected work years for each of these groups requires information on their likelihood of staying in service at each experience or year of service (YOS) level, on how proficiency grows with experience, and on the percentage of civilians who are veterans. We also use information on the percentage of military separations and retirements that are veteran civilian accessions. We computed average continuation rates by YOS for enlisted personnel who were cryptologic linguists from fiscal year (FY) 2000 to FY 2009 using monthly personnel records in the Proxy-Perstempo data provided by the Defense Manpower Data Center (DMDC). As described in Asch, Levy, and Krull (2009), these individuals are required to have language proficiency in order to be qualified in their occupation, and cryptologic linguists are the major source of military-provided language proficiency to the IC. We obtained information on average continuation rates by YOS for DoD civilians with at least a bachelor's degree from Gates et al. (2008). We find that, on average, an enlisted accession that becomes a cryptologic linguist provides 4.6 work years, while a DoD civilian accession provides 14.1 work years on average. The Gates study also provided information on the fraction of DoD civilian new hires that are former military personnel. The study's most recent estimate

---

[2]   In calculations not shown in the text, we considered the case where the comparison civilian workforce includes both veterans and nonveterans. Because the contributions of veterans and nonveterans are quite similar, we found that the results are quite similar to what we present in the main text, where the civilian workforce includes only nonveterans. We also considered the case where the comparison workforce includes all three types of personnel: veteran civilians, nonveteran civilians, and enlisted personnel. In this case, the net differences in the cost of providing a given level of proficiency are smaller than shown in the tables in this chapter, but the results are qualitatively the same: The comparison workforce is still more cost-effective than the military one. That the net differences are smaller is not surprising, given that in this alternative comparison the composition of the two workforces is more similar.

[3]   We could also include the contributions of nonveterans to the military workforce, but since their contributions would be entirely netted out when compared with the nonveteran civilian workforce, we exclude them.

is that about half of new hires in DoD are veterans. As described in the next subsection, we consider alternatives to this estimate as well. Finally, drawing on unpublished work by Bernard Rostker, we assume that veteran civilian accessions are 8 percent of military separations and retirements over three years, but we also consider an alternative to this estimate, as described in the next subsection.

Input on How Proficiency Grows with Experience

An input for computing proficiency-adjusted work years is an estimate of how language proficiency grows with experience, so that we can adjust expected work years by the amount of proficiency provided. We use information from our interviews regarding the proficiency levels of military and civilian personnel. Consider first enlisted personnel. As mentioned, proficiency for enlisted members is measured in terms of DLPT scores, where a level of 2/2 in listening and reading, respectively, means a test taker is rated as having limited working proficiency in each area. A level of 3/3 means that the test taker has general professional proficiency. We assumed, based on the interview input, that an enlisted member does not achieve a 2/2 level of proficiency until after completing two years of service, but that he or she reaches a 3/3 level by the eighth year of service. Thus, we assume a zero level of proficiency in YOS 1 and 2 for enlisted personnel, normalize their proficiency level to a value of 1 in YOS 3, increase the value linearly each year such that it is 1.2 in YOS 8, and keep the value at 1.2 level for the remainder of their careers. By "normalize," we mean that we use an index of how proficiency grows with experience, and we multiply the index at each YOS by the expected work years at that YOS. For example, the expected work years for enlisted cryptologic linguists at YOS 6 is 0.258, given continuation behavior through YOS 6. The proficiency index ay YOS 6 is 1.12, so proficiency-adjusted work years as of YOS 6 are 0.289. We sum across YOSs to compute expected proficiency-adjusted work years. We recognize that our approach for accounting for how proficiency grows with experience embeds some arbitrary assumptions, and we consider alternatives. As described in Appendix C, varying the assumption about how proficiency grows with experience has little effect on our overall results.

For both veteran and nonveteran civilians, we used two alternative approaches. In the first approach, we assume that civilian proficiency grows with YOS in an identical fashion to military personnel, with the exception that proficient work starts at entry, rather than in YOS 3.[4] For nonveteran civilians, this means that their index at YOS 1 equals 1. For veteran civilians, this means that their proficiency at entry equals what an enlisted member's would be after five years of service, given that expected years of service for a cryptologic linguist is 4.6 years (or 5, rounding up). The proficiency index for an enlisted member with five years of service (i.e., at YOS 6) is 1.12, so the proficiency index for veteran civilians at YOS 1 is 1.12. Thus, veteran civilians enter service with a proficiency advantage over nonveteran civilians, but the advantage is not permanent.

For the second approach, we assume that both veteran and nonveteran civilians have a higher level of proficiency than military personnel at YOS 1, consistent with what we heard in interviews. For the second approach, we assume that civilians enter with DLPT scores of 3/3 for listening and reading proficiency, regardless of their veteran's status, and that they maintain

---

[4] Unlike for military personnel, government civilians' language proficiency is currently not measured by DLPT scores but instead by other assessment tools. Since proficiency in the model is based on an assumed relationship, we measure proficiency in terms of DLPT for civilians and military personnel.

this level their entire career. Thus, the proficiency index starts at 1.2 at YOS 1 for both veterans and nonveterans and remains at that level the remainder of the career. We find that our results (not shown) differ a bit across the two cases, but not by much.

Computing Cost

Our computation of cost is guided by DoD DTM 09-007 and summarized in Table 3.1. For military personnel, we use cost elements for all enlisted personnel in FY 2011, not specifically language personnel, as referenced in DTM 09-007; but we use a different training cost estimate than the one referenced in DTM 09-007, because training costs for language training can be quite high relative to the average, and we also use different recruitment costs. Excluding training and recruitment costs, the average cost per work year to the government of an enlisted member is $102,090. As described in Appendix C, we use a rough estimate of $100,000 as the training cost per cryptologic linguist accession. This figure is rough but is likely to be conservative, because it will tend to favor military personnel (i.e., make military personnel relatively more cost-effective than they really are). We also consider alternative assumptions about training cost and recruitment cost, as we discuss shortly. Average recruitment costs per accession were obtained from the Office of Accession Policy within the Office of the Secretary of Defense for Personnel and Readiness. Averaging these costs over the period 2007–2011 in real 2011 dollars results in a figure of $19,600. For simplicity, we rounded this figure to $20,000 per enlisted accession.

To compute the cost of a workforce of enlisted personnel, we multiply the size of the (proficiency-unadjusted) workforce by $102,090 and multiply the number of accessions by the recruitment cost per accession and by the training cost per accession. The total is the cost of the enlisted workforce required to sustain a given level of proficiency (which we set at 2,000 work years for the purpose of this analysis).

To compute the cost of a workforce of veteran civilians, we use the cost elements listed in DTM 09-007 and in Table 3.1. For FY 2011, the average cost of a DoD civilian was $111,056. We multiply this average cost figure by the size of the veteran civilian workforce required to provide a given level of proficiency.

Similarly, to compute the cost of a workforce of nonveteran civilians, we multiply $111,056 by the size of the nonveteran workforce required to sustain that level of proficiency.

Finally, we compute the difference in cost per proficiency-adjusted work years. We compute the cost per proficiency-adjusted work year for military personnel, including both their contributions while enlisted and while employed as veteran civilians, and the cost per proficiency-adjusted work year for the comparison workforce of nonveteran civilians. This computation holds constant the number of proficiency work years provided by each personnel type, assumed to be 2,000. The difference in cost per work year is presented in the "Results" section of this chapter as the base case. We also consider several alternatives in the next section.

In sum, we compute the difference in the cost to the government of providing a fixed amount of proficiency by a military workforce and a civilian workforce, where the military workforce includes enlisted personnel and their expected work years if they join the civil service. Since we are considering cost differences, factors that are common to both workforces are netted out. Thus, the computation of cost differences only includes the marginal contribution of veteran civilians over nonveteran civilians, assumed to be short-lived because nonveteran civilians quickly catch up with veterans. As we will discuss later in this chapter, part of the cost difference between the military workforce and the civilian workforce is attributable to differences in the expected career lengths and therefore the expected workforces provided by enlisted personnel versus civilians. More enlisted accessions are needed to provide a given level of proficient work years because enlisted careers are much shorter and each military accession incurs a training and recruitment cost. Another factor is the relatively high cost of training military personnel, both in terms of the direct cost of training and the opportunity cost. The opportunity cost occurs because military personnel in training are not available to contribute to operations. A factor reducing the relative cost of military personnel is that we can spread the direct costs of training and recruiting military personnel over the work years provide by personnel while enlisted and years while they are veteran civil service employees. We present results on net costs later in the chapter, but first we discuss the cases we consider.

Other Cases We Analyze
The previous subsection provides information on the base case we consider. We also consider several alternatives we describe here. The alternatives allow us to examine scenarios that could have different policy implications from the base case and to examine the sensitivity of the results to alternative assumptions.

We consider two sets of alternatives. The first set explores the difference in cost per expected proficient work year when military personnel are able to gain proficiency earlier in their career, either because training time is shortened or because they enter the military already proficient. Thus, case 2 considers how the cost difference estimate changes when military personnel gain proficiency by the end of their first year rather than the end of their second. Such might be the situation for less-difficult languages for which training time is shorter, or because of possible efforts on the part of DoD to shorten course length through improved training methods, or because of possible efforts to recruit more proficient recruits or recruits who acquire language capability faster. In this case, training costs are assumed to be $75,000 rather than $100,000. Case 3 considers the case where the military is able to recruit enlisted personnel who are fully proficient at entry and require minimal language training, though they would still require cryptologic training. This case assumes that these policies would reduce training costs in the model from $100,000 to $50,000 per recruit, as described in Appendix C. The approach in case 3 could also impose new costs, however. For example, higher enlistment bonuses would likely be required to recruit proficient enlisted personnel or personnel who can acquire language rapidly. We therefore assume in case 3 that the average recruitment costs increase to $40,000.

The results from the first set of alternatives permit us to gain some insight into whether shortening training length would impart a cost savings relative to the base case and whether the cost difference would be appreciably affected if military personnel attain proficiency earlier in their career. While the policy analysis is exploratory, a finding that the relative cost-effectiveness of military personnel is affected by amount of training would suggest exploring further the possibility of reducing training time for military personnel.

The second set of alternatives we consider explores differences in cost per work year when the flow of veterans to the civil service varies from what is assumed in the base case. As mentioned, available data indicate that a large number of civilian accessions are former military personnel, though we do not have information specific to the language community in the IC. A consistent theme we heard in the interviews was the importance of veterans to some IC missions requiring language capability. A question of interest is what would happen to the relative cost of using military personnel if the flow were reduced or, alternatively, increased. Would the cost difference between military and civilian personnel change substantially? Would there be substantial cost savings from using enlisted personnel relative to the base case? While the analysis is exploratory, it can provide some insights into the importance of not just the federal government's policy preference for veterans, but other incentives and programs that make federal service attractive to veterans.

To account for differences in the flow to the civil service, case 4 assumes that the flow is zero, i.e., no veteran joins the civil service and all civilian accessions are nonveteran accessions. In contrast, case 5 assumes that the flow is 75 percent, i.e., 75 percent of civilian accessions are veterans, and case 5 assumes that 32 percent of enlisted veterans would join the civil service, instead of 8 percent in the base case. As we will show in the discussion of results in the next section, of critical importance to the relative cost-effectiveness of military personnel is not the percentage of civilians who are hired, which is rather high at 50 percent in our analysis, but the percentage of veterans who are hired as civilians, which is quite low at 8 percent in our analysis. The analysis of these alternatives also allows us to examine the sensitivity of the results to different assumptions.

Results

Table 5.1 shows the results of each case. The top panel of the table shows the work year, accessions, and cost per proficiency-adjusted work years for the military workforce, which consists of enlisted personnel and veteran civilian personnel. The middle panel shows these calculations for the civilian workforce composed of nonveterans. The bottom panel shows the key results of interest, the different or net cost per proficiency-adjusted workforce of the military workforce relative to the civilian workforce. A positive difference means that the military workforce is relatively more costly from a government-wide perspective, holding constant the number of proficient work years. Every case holds proficiency work years constant at 2,000.[5]

In the base case (case 1), the cost of the military workforce (consisting of enlisted personnel and veteran civilians) is $127,242 per proficient work year. Enlisted personnel contribute 1,187 work years; after adjusting for proficiency, this figure is 904. Given the retention rates of cryptologic linguists and the assumed relationship between proficiency and experience, we find it takes 260 accessions to provide those work years. The average cost per proficient work year of the enlisted workforce is $168,603. Veteran civilians provide the remaining 1,096 proficiency-adjusted work years (2,000 – 904). Given the continuation behavior of civilians and the assumed relationship between proficiency and experience, it takes 65 accessions to provide the 1,096 proficiency-adjusted work years. The average cost of a civilian veteran is $93,128. The comparison group is the nonveteran civilian workforce, and we find that the cost of this workforce is $95,001 per proficient work year, where 2,000 proficient work years are provided. Sustaining this workforce requires 121 accessions per year. The average cost per proficient work year for nonveteran civilian personnel is a bit more than that for veteran civilian personnel ($95,001 versus $93,128) because we assume that veteran civilians enter the civil service with slightly greater proficiency for IC missions than nonveterans, though this advantage is not permanent.

---

[5]   The proficiency-adjusted number for the civilian workforce is 2,000 but, as shown at the top of the table, it varies between 1,998 to 2,002 for the military workforce. Thus, the number is not exactly 2,000, but is close.

Table 5.1
Results of Exploratory Model

	Base Case	Enlisted Proficient After YOS 1	Enlisted Proficient at Entry (and Enlistment Bonus)	No Flow of Enlisted to Civilian Workforce	75% of Civilian Accessions Are Veterans, 32% of Enlisted Veterans Are Hired as Civilians
	(1)	(2)	(3)	(4)	(5)
Military Workforce (enlisted + veteran civilian)					
Total proficiency-adjusted work years	2,000	2,002	1,998	2,001	2,002
Total cost per proficient work year	$127,242	$113,290	$102,063	$168,773	$108,596
Enlisted personnel					
Work years	1,187	1,091	991	2,630	470
Proficiency-adjusted work years	904	1,007	1,104	2,001	358
Required accessions	260	239	217	576	103
Total cost per proficient work year	$168,603	$133,208	$109,292	$168,773	$168,773
Veteran civilian personnel					
Work years	919	834	749	N/A	1,379
Proficiency-adjusted work years	1,096	995	894	N/A	1,644
Required accessions	65	59	53	N/A	97.5
Total cost per proficient work year	$93,128	$93,128	$93,128	N/A	$93,128
Civilian Workforce (nonveteran)					
Work years	1,711	1,711	1,711	1,711	1,711
Proficiency-adjusted work years	2,000	2,000	2,000	2,000	2,000
Required accessions	121	121	121	121	121
Total cost per proficient work year	$95,001	$95,001	$95,001	$95,001	$95,001
Difference between military workforce and civilian workforce cost per proficient work year	$32,241	$18,228	$7,061	$73,772	$13,595

NOTE: Costs are in FY 2011 dollars.

Accounting for the contribution of veterans affects cost per proficient work years for the military workforce in several ways. First, because veterans contribute work years to proficiency, fewer enlisted accessions are required to sustain 2,000 proficient work years. This is seen by comparing enlisted accessions in the base case (260) to enlisted accessions in case 4 (576), where we assume no flow of veterans to the civil service. Second, the fixed costs associated with using enlisted personnel are spread over the years contributed by veteran civilians. The total cost per proficient work year for the military force (including enlisted personnel and veteran civilians) is $127,242. This figure is substantially lower than $168,603 because the high training costs of $100,000 per accession and recruitment costs of $20,000 per accession drives up the average cost of an enlisted member. When these costs are partially spread over the 1,096 proficient years provided by veterans, the average cost is reduced.

In the base case, we find that military personnel are a more costly means of providing a given level of proficiency to the government (2,000 in our model). The bottom panel shows the difference in cost per proficient work year. Specifically, enlisted personnel are $32,241 more costly per work year provided than civilian personnel in the base case. Assuming a less conservative level of training costs (not shown), e.g., a figure higher than $100,000, increases the relative cost of military personnel, making them even less cost-effective. Alternative assumptions about how proficiency grows with experience have little effect on the overall conclusion that military personnel are less cost-effective than civilian personnel. Furthermore, this conclusion is consistent with what we heard in the interviews we conducted about the value to the IC language mission of depth of knowledge and experience, factors that favor the civilian workforce.

Of course, the cost of providing a given level of proficiency is not the only consideration in weighing the benefits and costs of a military versus civilian workforce. Other considerations include the need for military-specific knowledge and skills, the ability to deploy military personnel and use them in dangerous situations, the ability to generate a large flow of language personnel through the DLIFLC pipeline, and the benefits to the military that come from having some military personnel support strategic missions, such as those at NSA/CSS. That military personnel are more expensive, according to the exploratory model, means that these other considerations yield benefits that outweigh the additional costs. Measuring these benefits are outside the scope of this analysis but should be considered in any workforce mix decision.

It is important to reiterate that the results are from the standpoint of the government as a whole. A specific agency, such as NSA/CSS, may not consider the contribution of enlisted personnel to DoD when these personnel are used in operational units, nor does a specific agency generally bear the full cost associated with using or training these personnel. Thus, from the standpoint of a specific agency, military personnel may be relatively more cost-effective than civilians, even though our analysis suggests that they are less cost-effective from a government-wide perspective.

We find that the cost advantage of civilian personnel is smaller when military personnel require less language training, and it almost disappears when they require no language training. This is seen in cases 2 and 3 in Table 5.1. Shortening the training time to one year, versus two years in the base case, increases the cost-effectiveness of military personnel such that the difference falls to $18,228, given our modeling assumptions. That is, military personnel cost $18,228 more per work year than civilians, holding proficiency constant. Eliminating language training further reduces the cost advantage of civilians to $7,061, given our assumptions.

The cost-effectiveness of military personnel increases when they require less language training for two reasons. First, enlisted personnel provide more work years because less time is spent in training and more time in support of operational mission requirements. This is seen by comparing the number of enlisted accessions and the number of adjusted work years in case 3 versus the base case. Fewer accessions (217 versus 260) are required to sustain more proficient adjusted work years (1,104 versus 904). Second, training costs are lower, from $100,000 to $50,000 per accession, by assumption, because enlisted personnel spend less time in classroom training.

This analysis suggests that higher language-training costs for enlisted personnel versus civilian personnel are an important reason for the relatively higher cost of military personnel to the government. Lowering training times for enlisted personnel could be a means of reducing the relative cost of military personnel. For example, the IC could concentrate the use of military personnel in missions that require less proficiency in difficult languages or that require proficiency in languages that are less difficult for English-speakers to learn, such as Spanish. These approaches would reduce language-training time and reduce the training cost per accession. Another approach would be to recruit more intensively people who already have proficiency in required languages. For example, the services might recruit more intensively in heritage communities. Of course, doing so could increase recruitment costs, because these individuals may be difficult to find and/or have greater difficulty meeting other enlistment standards, such as citizenship standards. We incorporate higher recruitment costs in our analysis of case 3 and find that the cost advantage of civilians is substantially reduced relative to the base case when military personnel do not require training. However, our analysis does not incorporate the cost of substantially revamping and changing the language-training curriculum for military personnel to incorporate such changes. Those costs could make military personnel more expensive. Still, these are likely to be fixed costs that could be amortized over time, though they could represent substantial budgetary costs in any given budget year. In sum, the analysis suggests that military personnel are relatively more cost-effective when training times are lower, compared with nonveteran civilians. Further analysis would be required to investigate the feasibility of alternative policies to reduce training times.

Consideration of cases 4 and 5 suggest that the size of the flow of military personnel to the civil service, relative to overall civilian accessions, is another factor explaining the higher cost of military personnel in providing a given level of proficiency. We find that when there is no flow to the civil service (case 4), the relative cost of military personnel more than doubles, from $32,241 in the base case to $73,772. The reason is that enlisted personnel provide far fewer work years per accession given their continuation rates (4.6 versus 14.1), so far more military accessions are required to sustain 2,000 proficiency-adjusted work years (576 versus 260 in the base case). More accessions must be recruited and trained, such that the total cost of training and recruiting the military workforce to achieve those 2,000 years is much higher. Furthermore, because there are no veteran civilians in case 4, the higher training and recruitment costs of enlisted personnel are spread only across the years they provide while they are in military service and not the years they might have served as civilians.

In contrast, when the flow of enlisted personnel to the civil service is much greater, constituting 75 percent of civilian accessions and 32 rather than 8 percent of military separations (case 5), the cost advantage of civilians is reduced to $13,595. When more enlisted personnel also serve as veteran civilians, fewer enlisted accessions are required (103 accessions versus 260 in the base case). Veterans provide more work years (1,644 versus 1,096), so the fixed training and recruitment costs of employing enlisted personnel are spread over more veteran work years. While it is still the case that military personnel are more costly relative to nonveteran civilians, given our model assumptions, they are less costly than when the flow to the civil service is lower. Of critical importance to this result is the percentage of veterans who are hired (32 percent in case 5 versus 8 percent in the base case). In analysis not shown in the table, we also considered the case where the percentage of civilian hires that are veteran is 75 percent, but only 8 percent of veterans are hired. We find little change in the relative cost-effectiveness of military personnel relative to the base case. This result suggests that what drives the improvement in the cost-effectiveness of military personnel when the flow of veteran hires is increased is not the increase in the percentage of civilian hires that are veteran (the change from 50 percent to 75 percent) but rather the increase in the percentage of veterans that are hired (from 8 percent to 32 percent). The hiring rate among veterans is critical because this factor determines the degree to which the high cost of language training for military personnel can be spread over their civilian careers.

The analysis suggests that the IC might be able to enhance the net return to the government from training and recruiting military language professionals by increasing the hiring rate of veterans. Policies that increase the flow of veterans to the civil service and the recruitment of trained veterans, such as "veterans preferences" in federal hiring decisions, might improve the cost-effectiveness of military personnel relative to the comparison group of nonveteran civilians, as would programs that provide guidance to veteran language personnel to pursue careers in the IC as language professionals. Doing so would potentially involve greater cost, such as the cost of recruitment bonuses for civilians. Our analysis of case 5 included a $40,000 recruitment bonus for civilian veterans. That said, military personnel remain more costly to the government even in this case, so that the advantages of using military personnel, such as their specialized knowledge and skills, and the other factors that we do not incorporate into our analysis must also be weighed in the workforce mix decision.

Summary

We developed an exploratory model of the relative cost to the government of providing the same amount of language capability to an IC mission using a military workforce versus a civilian one. We account for the flow of military personnel who later become civilian language professionals, so the military workforce comprises both enlisted personnel while in the military and civilians who are former enlisted personnel. Thus, the military workforce is actually a mix of enlisted and veteran civilians, and is compared against a workforce that consist of only nonveteran civilians. Since we consider the relative cost-effectiveness of these groups, we measure the net cost or difference in cost per proficient work year; to the extent that there are similarities between the contribution of veterans and nonveterans, these are netted out. Put differently, the metric of relative cost-effectiveness only considers the marginal contribution of veterans to the military workforce.[6] The model is exploratory because we use data on all enlisted and all DoD civilians, not data specific to language professionals or the IC, with the exception of continuation rate data specific to enlisted cryptologic linguists. Still, the analysis provides a first look at the relative cost-effectiveness of military versus nonveteran civilian language professionals. That said, our framework indicates that a multitude of factors are important in assessing the best mix of personnel, not just relative cost-effectiveness.

We find that the nonveteran civilian workforce is relatively more cost-effective in providing a given level of language capability, given our assumptions and our government-wide perspective. Our estimated cost savings are probably underestimated, because we assume the average enlisted training cost is around $100,000, whereas our interviews as well as the training cost information we received from DLIFLC suggest that training costs far exceed this figure. We also assume that half of civilian accessions are veterans and that 8 percent of military veterans (over a three-year period) are civilian accessions. If these figures are lower than 50 percent

---

[6]   While we could include veterans in the civilian workforce comparison group, we would then have to also include their contributions when they had been in the military, in which case our comparison group would be little different (if at all) from the military group. We could also include nonveterans to the military workforce, but since their contributions would be entirely netted out when compared with the nonveteran civilian workforce, we exclude them.

and 8 percent, the relative cost advantage of civilians is even greater. In fact, when we consider zero flow from the enlisted force to the civil service, the relative cost of a military workforce is more than twice that of the civilian workforce.

The analysis provides some insight into why civilians appear relatively more cost-effective to the government. The average cost of a civilian is not much different from the average cost of enlisted members over their career. Instead, much of the cost savings stems from the fact that military personnel rarely enter service with language proficiency, and so must be trained in language, and they receive basic training and training in cryptologic skills. Not only is training costly in terms of the cost of putting a student through DLIFLC, but the opportunity cost of training is also high. Military personnel who are in training are not available to provide operational support to missions. Another reason for the cost advantage of civilians is that they stay in service longer and their expected number of work years per accession is far higher than it is for enlisted personnel. This effect is partly offset by the flow of veterans to the civilian workforce. Thus, part of the return to military service occurs when personnel leave and enter the civilian workforce. However, this effect is not large enough to fully offset the shorter number of work years provided by personnel while they are enlisted. Even when we consider a case where 75 percent of civilian accessions are veterans and 32 percent of veterans are hired as civilians over a three-year period, we still find that nonveteran civilians are relatively more cost-effective.

The results of the qualitative analysis are suggestive and provide guidance on areas that would be fruitful to consider further. Specifically, the analysis suggests that reducing training time for military personnel could improve their cost-effectiveness, as would increasing the flow of veterans to the civil service. We discuss these themes more in the next chapter.

CHAPTER SIX

Summary and Concluding Thoughts

This chapter summarizes our key findings and offers some concluding thoughts about the factors affecting the best workforce of language professionals in the IC. In the process, we also discuss our framework for assessing workforce mix and offer some thoughts about potential areas for improving the management of language professionals in the IC.

Factors to Consider in Assessing Workforce Mix

DoD guidance and policy provides a useful starting point for assessing the best workforce mix of military, government civilian, and contractor personnel. The NSA/CSS, the agency that we considered as a case study in our qualitative analysis, is a DoD agency, so DoD guidance is relevant. Currently, ODNI does not have similar guidance, and DoD guidance could be a useful template to begin formulating similar ODNI guidance on workforce mix. We supplemented DoD guidance with information garnered from a review of the economics and management literature, focusing on the factors that drive cost or benefits.

DoD guidance focuses on ensuring that defense missions are executed with limited risk, with risk mitigation taking precedence of cost-effectiveness. Contractors are not permitted to perform activities intimately related to the public interest—so-called inherently governmental activities—or personal services or activities that are precluded from commercial performance due to law or executive order. In general, government employees are the preferred source of manpower, according to DoD guidance, with military manpower preferred over civilians when military personnel are required for readiness or workforce needs. If no such needs are present, then civilians are the preferred source of manpower unless a cost analysis indicates that they are relatively more costly.

The economics literature and past studies suggest that personnel costs and benefits reflect productivity differences, which, in turn, are affected by differences in education, experience, training (including in language skills), and other factors that lead to differences in knowledge, skill, and ability. Productivity also increases with work effort and performance incentives, technology, the operational environment, and the type and extent of complementary skills. Collateral duties can reduce availability by drawing away effort and attention, while such factors as corporate culture help standardize procedures, smooth communication, and improve processes and productivity. On the other hand, constraints that limit the flexible use of personnel hurt productivity and drive up costs. Miscellaneous factors, such as contractual-related costs, e.g., the cost of specifying all contingencies and what actions are required under each contingency, reduce the effectiveness and increase the cost of using contractors.

It is clear that an array of factors are relevant to workforce mix decisions. Some of these factors are amenable to measurement, while others are not. Therefore, to assess these factors in the context of language workforce mix decisions in the IC, we took a qualitative and quantitative approach. Because we focused only on one agency, the NSA/CSS, in our qualitative analysis and did not use IC-specific data for language personnel in our quantitative analysis, our approach should be considered a first look and exploratory. Nonetheless, the quantitative and qualitative approaches are complementary and provide some insights into workforce mix considerations and potential areas for improved management. We summarize these insights next.

Workforce Mix Considerations

The insights from the interviews, together with the results of our exploratory modeling analysis, support some broad observations about the factors contributing to the best mix of various categories of personnel (military personnel, government civilians, and contractors) providing language capability in the IC, particularly NSA/CSS. We reiterate that we take a government-wide perspective and that the perspective of an individual agency might lead to different results, since the costs and benefits of using different categories of personnel will be different for a specific agency than for the government as a whole. Furthermore, because we take a government-wide rather than an agency perspective, implementation could be challenging because individual agencies may not be able or willing to make decisions that lead to the best mix from a government-wide perspective. We do not address the implementation issues in this study but recognize their importance. Thus, our conclusions are broad statements rather than specific policy guidelines.

The most important overarching observation is that each category of personnel provides unique advantages and belongs in the "workforce mix." Together, the analysis suggests that the IC should consider the following steps in planning future workforce mix for providing language capability, though additional information would be required on the feasibility and effectiveness of these steps for specific missions:

- Plan to use all three sources.
- Build core-staffing requirements around permanent civilian positions. As mentioned, there is a general perception, though by no means universal, that NSA/CSS needs more civilians providing language capability.
- Continue to invest resources in developing and training military personnel to support current missions and as a source of future civilian staff.
- Continue to use contractors to augment and extend the civilian and military workforce; further explore their potential value as a "pipeline" for future permanent civilian staff.

Civilians are the "backbone" of the language function in the IC. The interviews revealed that, compared with enlisted personnel, they are more experienced, better educated, have greater language proficiency and deeper target knowledge, provide continuity, and bring other requisite capabilities, including writing skills, analytic skills and supervisory and mentoring capabilities. Furthermore, our modeling analysis suggests that a workforce of nonveteran civilian language professions is a relatively more cost-effective way to provide language capability to the government than a military one comprising enlisted personnel and veteran civilians. That said, because our model is exploratory, additional analysis that is specific to the function under consideration should verify this finding.

This does not mean that the analysis implies that IC language missions should be staffed only by civilian language professionals. Interviewees told us that military personnel bring unique knowledge, especially to missions requiring understanding of military tactics and the operational environment. Functional managers told us that military personnel, while generally young and in their first assignment, can be successfully mentored and developed over time. Furthermore, we were told that they provide a "farm team" for the civilian workforce and that DLIFLC is a unique resource that can provide a large and steady stream of trained language professionals to the IC. Assignments at NSA/CSS also benefit the military by allowing military personnel to develop and use their language skills, providing them with a "big picture" of the national mission and, more pragmatically, a list of "who to call at NSA/CSS" when they return to their service mission and are in the field with questions.

We were also told that contractors also have unique advantages, especially the ability to provide surge capability at NSA/CSS, though contractors providing language capability at NSA/CSS are relatively rare. They enable managers to meet short-run requirements or requirements for highly specialized skills, such as less-used dialects. Contractors also provide a "farm team" for the civilian workforce and often consist of former military personnel who have recently left service. Contractors who are native speakers, however, may have difficultly getting cleared at the requisite levels and may have difficulties with English language proficiency. On the other hand, interviewees indicated that because contractors focus only on their work, with no collateral duties, and they can be fired relatively more easily, they may have stronger performance incentives, though we were unable to include contractors in our model.

Workforce Management Issues

While the focus of the analysis was on workforce mix, we were able to make some observations, informed by the people we interviewed, about issues and possible recommendations for improving the management of military and civilian language professionals. First, interviewees repeatedly told us that DoD and the military services should consider placing greater emphasis on optimizing the use of language over the military career and ensuring the career development of skilled language professionals for the benefit of the defense and intelligence communities. Some suggested that this should include a closer look at the possibility of creating a career path for military language professionals that deviates from the typical enlisted career. For example, several interviewees suggests that DoD might consider making language professionals a warrant officer field, thereby allowing even mid-career and senior personnel to provide language capability in addition to being supervisors and leaders. Alternatively, like other "excepted communities," such as pilots, chaplains, and health professionals, uniformed language professionals might be a separate competitive category of service. These suggestions are currently relevant to officers but were suggested even for enlisted personnel. Some argued that these alternative career paths would allow military language professionals to focus on developing and using language, would enable community managers to promote personnel in part based on language capability, and might reduce the collateral duties that currently divert the effort of military language personnel away from providing language capability. That said, additional analysis is required to assess these claims, including the feasibility and effectiveness of these policies.

Our exploratory analysis of the relative cost-effectiveness of a military versus nonveteran civilian language workforce revealed that recruiting military personnel who lack language proficiency and training them, which often takes long periods of time, dramatically increases the relative cost of military personnel and puts them at a cost disadvantage relative to nonveteran civilians. The analysis suggests that recruiting military personnel who are proficient, or who require less extensive and time-consuming training, might reduce the cost to the government of using military personnel to provide language proficiency to the IC. While additional analysis is needed about the most cost-effective and appropriate way to recruit language proficient enlistees, past research of the effects of recruiting policy suggest that incentives, such as bonuses and educational benefits, might be a promising approach.

The exploratory analysis also revealed that accounting for the contribution of civilians who are former military personnel and the flow of military personnel to the civil service is important to the assessment of relative cost-effectiveness to the government. While the estimate of the net cost of the military workforce includes only the marginal contribution of veterans, we find that failure to account for this contribution tends to result in an overstatement of the relative cost of a work year provided by military personnel versus nonveteran civilians. In large part, this is due to the ability to spread the fixed costs, notably training and recruitment costs, of enlisted personnel over the expected work years provided by veterans. DoD guidance should consider instructing personnel managers conducting workforce mix studies to account for this flow to more accurately assess relative cost-effectiveness, both in terms of the percentage of military separations that enter the civil service and the percentage of hires that are veterans. Our analysis uses 8 percent for the first figure and 50 percent for the second, but personnel managers should use the actual data to compute the relevant figure for their workforce. Such an analysis should also recognize the cost of any policy to generate a flow of veterans to the civil service. Furthermore, the analysis suggests that the greater the flow, the smaller the cost advantage of civilians over the military workforce. That said, even when we considered a case where three-quarters of civilian accessions were veterans and nearly a third of military separations over three years were hired as civilians, we still found that civilians were relatively more cost-effective, even after incorporating a civilian recruitment bonus. Nonetheless, the exploratory analysis suggests that DoD and the IC might consider more actively encouraging this flow. Currently, veterans are giving preference in civilian hiring. However, the preference is not contingent on skill. Civilian managers of functions where military knowledge is important might consider offering higher recruitment bonuses to veterans with language skills. Policymakers in the IC concerned with language capability might also consider career guidance material targeted to trained military personnel to encourage their employment as civilian language professionals in the IC.

Policymakers should reconsider the constraints on hiring civilians, such as the authorization and appropriations processes, so that workforce managers can optimize the mix of personnel, including the hiring and employment of government civilians.

On net, our assessment indicates that all personnel categories contribute language capability to the IC. Different missions often require different language skills as well as other complementary skills, knowledge, and abilities. Furthermore, different missions embody different risks and are conducted in different operational contexts. Consequently, there is no simple rule of thumb for deciding workforce mix. Each mission requires a careful analysis of the array of factors discussed in this report.

Details on DoD Guidance of Workforce Mix

This appendix offers greater detail on the guidance and criteria provided by DoD for the appropriate mix of personnel, which was summarized in Chapter Two.

The overarching guiding principle is that national military objectives should be accomplished with a minimum of manpower, organized and employed to provide maximum effectiveness and combat power. DoD Directive 1100.4, *Guidance for Manpower Management*, states that manpower management should be flexible, both adaptive to program changes and responsive to crisis situations. This directive also states that missions should be accomplished using the least costly mix of personnel, consistent with military requirements and other needs of DoD. This chapter summarizes the specific guidance and criteria given by DoD in DoDI 1100.22, DoD Directive 1100.4, and elsewhere to determine the mix of military personnel, government civilians, and contractors to perform DoD activities and tasks.

Although cost-effectiveness is a criterion for determining the mix, the DoD instructions provide no specific information on why different factors affect cost or benefits. To fill this gap, Chapter Three draws from the past defense manpower literature, as well as the economics and management literature, to address the issue of factors related to cost-effectiveness and why they are important. In this appendix, we focus on the criteria for determining the mix based on DoD guidance.

DoDI 1100.22 first identifies the criteria that exempt an activity from performance by the private sector, and in the process provides guidance on the choice of military versus civilian manpower. Thus, the instruction implies that in the absence of an exemption, DoD functions and activities should be performed by the private sector. The DoD instruction then cites an earlier directive (DoD Directive 1100.4, *Guidance for Manpower Management*) to state that if an activity is exempt from private-sector performance, it should be designated as civilian unless there are exceptions that indicate the need to perform the activity with military personnel. Thus, given the decision to perform "in-house," the activity or function should be performed by civilians rather than military personnel, unless one of the exceptions is relevant.

Below, we summarize and discuss the criteria listed in DoDI 1100.22 for exempting performance by the private sector and for designating performance by the military. We first focus on the criteria and factors that lead to exemption from private-sector performance. We then focus the discussion on the criteria and factors that lead to the designation of a function or task as military rather than civilian.

Exemptions from Private-Sector Performance: Criteria for "In-House" Performance

Factors that exempt performance by the private sector and therefore lead to guidance to perform the function by government personnel are listed in Table A.1. Each of these factors is discussed in this subsection. As will be clear in the discussion of the factors, some of the exemptions favor the designation of activities or tasks as military, while others favor civilian personnel.

Table A.1
Factors That Exempt Performance by the Private Sector

Inherently governmental
Operational risk
Wartime assignments
Esprit de corps
Continuity of operations
Rotation
Career progression
Law, executive order, treaty, international agreement
Management decision

The criteria in Table A.1 have a specific order of precedence, designated by a letter, shown in Table A.2. Specifically, criterion A takes first precedence over all other criteria, while criterion M has the lower precedence of the criteria listed. As described in DoDI 1100.22, the ordering is to give visibility to the reasons why activities should be performed by civilians or military personnel. Manpower managers are required to indicate the criteria when documenting manpower mix decisions.

Inherently Governmental

The first exemption in Table A.1 is whether a function or task is "inherently governmental." In Table A.2, criteria A, E, F, and I identify activities that are inherently governmental. The instruction states that these are "activities that require the exercise of discretion when applying Federal Government authority or value judgments when making decisions for the Federal Government" and indicates that the definition of inherently governmental should be consistent with the U.S. Code, OMB Circular A-76, the FAR, and other regulations. The OMB Circular A-76 definition of inherently governmental is "an activity that is so intimately related to the public interest as to mandate performance by government personnel."[1]

The instruction provides a detailed list of criteria for determining whether a task or function is inherently governmental. In general, these are tasks and activities that require discretion or decisionmaking authority, that might give rise to conflict of interest if performed by a contractor, that are performed in a hostile setting or require the command and control of military

---

[1] The Congressional Research Service recently issued a report that provides detailed background on the definition of *inherently governmental* within the Department of Defense (Congressional Research Service, June 2009). The quote from the OMB Circular A-76 is taken from the CRS report (p. 17).

Table A.2
Order of Precedence for Factors That Exempt Performance by the Private Sector

A. Direction and control of combat and crisis situations (inherently governmental)

B. Combat support and combat service support due to operational risk

D. Manpower dual-tasked for wartime assignments

E. DoD civilian authority, direction and control (inherently governmental)

F. Military unique knowledge and skills (inherently governmental)

G. Esprit de corps

H. Continuity of infrastructure operations

I. Military augmentation of the infrastructure during war (inherently governmental)

J. Civilian and military rotation

K. Civilian and military career progression

L. Law, executive order, treaty, or international agreement

M. DoD management decision

NOTE: There is no "C" criteria in DoDI 1100.22.

forces, that require unique military knowledge and skills, or that require the continuity provided by government manpower in a crisis situation.

The first criterion for determining whether an activity is inherently governmental is direction and control of combat and crisis situations. These activities and tasks include the operational command and control of military forces, authority over military discipline and the Uniform Code of Military Justice, and command and control over combat operations. Because military personnel can by ordered to perform their duties and are not permitted to quit, they provide military commanders with the control and flexibility to quickly reassign personnel, reconstitute operations, and provide assistance during hostilities. Thus, military discipline enables commanders to respond effectively in crises, and such discipline is inherently governmental. Also included under the "direction and control" are functions and activities that involve security provided to protect resources in a hostile area, criminal justice, law enforcement, interrogations performed in an operational environment, medical and chaplain services in hostile areas, and other support functions in an operational environment.

The second criterion for determining if a function is inherently governmental is whether it is related to DoD civilian authority, direction, and control. If it is, civilians are usually the appropriate choice, though cases exist where members of the military perform these functions. These tasks include judgments related to monetary transactions; the acquisition and use of property; the authority to obligate federal funds, conduct foreign relations, recommend and respond to Congress, and determine policies, directives, and regulations; approval of strategic plans; determination of program priorities; discretionary decisions about the effective and efficient organization, administration, and operation of DoD; and direction and control of certain functions, such as intelligence and counterintelligence operations, criminal investigations, and employee relations.

Use of civilians may also be favored in situations in which functions are inherently governmental and civilian experience and expertise are needed to make informed decisions, preclude the sole reliance on contractors, and enable DoD to maintain ultimate control and accountability of governmental operations, federally funded projects, contracts, and government property. While contractors can assist in performing these functions and tasks, they cannot perform tasks that involve discretion and control.

The third criterion for determining whether a function is inherently governmental activity is whether it is related to the unique knowledge, skills, and abilities of military personnel. These tasks are those that require "military advice and counsel" to the President, Congress, the National Security Council, Secretary of Defense, senior DoD officials or Secretaries, and the Joint Chiefs and the Combatant Commanders. They also include tasks that are required for the accomplishment of military missions, military justice, law enforcement under the Uniform Code of Military Justice, and administration of military confinement facilities. These tasks may also be designated for military performance if they involve the authority to commit DoD to take actions by direction, order, policy, regulation, contract, or regulation, and the work involved requires military-unique knowledge and skills.

The instruction also lists functions and tasks that require knowledge and skills unique to the military that facilitate DoD's ability to maintain control and accountability of government operations, projects, contracts, property, and funds. Military personnel can ensure that DoD officials are ". . . properly connected to the war-fighting establishment and are aware of the war-fighter's perspective on programs and actions intended to support military operations. They perform a discretionary role in establishing objectives, setting priorities, assessing alternatives, judging risks, and deciding the course of action on military-related matters."

These tasks and functions include those that determine the operational requirements and gaps in military capabilities and that require military knowledge and skills acquired by recent assignments in the operating forces. They may include basic training and the military training of doctrine and tactics, or training intended to acculturate military personnel. Other tasks may include the performance of research, development, testing, and evaluation where the work requires judgments based on military knowledge and skills, such as the potential use of emerging technologies and strategies for integrating new systems on the battlefield or the fleet. Tasks requiring military knowledge and skills also include intelligence and counterintelligence operations if they require substantial discretion, as well as tasks involving the handling of enemy prisoners of war, terrorists, and other detainees. Finally, tasks requiring manpower to provide advisory assistance and support on defense-related matters on behalf of DoD to agencies outside of DoD or to international organizations and foreign nations are also considered inherently governmental and are required to be performed by military personnel.

The final criterion that defines a task or function as inherently governmental is if it is performed by military personnel who are reassigned to operating units and their vacated positions require military knowledge and skills. Also, manpower that is needed, not just to backfill positions, but to augment infrastructure activities during a war, crisis, or mobilization due to an increased workload, are to be designated as military if they require military knowledge and skills.

Operational Risk

The instruction identifies exemptions from private performance based on operational risk. Some of these risks require performance of these functions by military personnel, while other risks allow performance by civilians.

The instruction states that manpower authorities should designate military personnel to perform a task or function, even if military capability is not normally required for proper performance of the function, if performance by civilians or contractors would constitute an unacceptable risk. Situations where there is significant risk and therefore require military capability include those where the threat level could increase and military personnel would be needed on short notice or where civilians or contractors may choose to quit because of the threat level or duration of the hostilities. In contrast, military personnel are subject to the Uniform Code of Justice and are subject to criminal prosecution if they choose not to perform their duties in a hostile environment.

Similarly, civilians should be designated to perform a task or function if a military capability is not normally required to perform the duty and reliance on a contractor would constitute an unacceptable risk. Specifically, the instruction identifies emergency civilian personnel who provide continuity for essential functions, maintain combat essential systems, or perform duties critical to combat operations in overseas locations during a crisis.

Wartime Assignments

According to DoD Directive 1100.4, manpower authorities must establish enough manpower in the DoD infrastructure to ensure that there is an adequate pool of personnel available to fill critical assignments in the operating forces during a mobilization, crisis, or war. Consequently, they must identify civilians and military personnel in the infrastructure who are performing commercial activities in peacetime but who would be needed for wartime assignments in the operating forces or would serve as replacements for personnel in the operating forces during wartime or mobilization. These personnel are "dual-tasked" because in wartime they are assigned to the operating forces but are not assigned to the operating forces in peacetime. These peacetime assignments in the infrastructure are exempt from performance by the private sector, even if the activity is a commercial activity that could be performed by a contractor in other circumstances.

Esprit de Corps

Manpower managers can exempt commercial activities that foster public support for DoD and help in meeting recruiting and retention goals. The "esprit de corps" exemption is intended to demonstrate DoD's commitment to military personnel and to engender group spirit and a sense of pride. Activities included under this exemption are the military bands and honor guards, the Navy Blue Angels, the superintendents of the military academies, and a subset of military recruiters.

Continuity of Operations

Manpower authorities can exempt activities and tasks to ensure the continuity of operations during a national emergency or war and during peacetime. During wartime or a national emergency, key civilian or military personnel may be incapacitated or reassigned to other functions. Thus, the government must conserve enough "mass" to continue to perform its essential functions.

During peacetime operations, manpower authorities must ensure sufficient manpower to continue operations when personnel transfer in and out of the activity. Thus, manpower should be designated as civilian when there is high turnover of personnel due to rotation or career progression.

Manpower can also be designated as civilian if the manpower must be needed as a ready and controlled source of technical or professional expertise, i.e., a core capability, to quickly respond to surges in the inherently governmental workforce, to respond to emergency situations, to enable managers to more effectively manage or control work associated with inherently governmental functions so that missions are not put at risk, or to ensure an effective and timely response to a mobilization, war, or other emergency.

Rotation

Manpower authorities are required to provide a rotation base for overseas and sea-to-shore rotation. Thus, manpower performing work that could be considered for private-sector performance can be designated as exempt from private-sector performance if the positions are needed to provide a rotation base for civilians outside of the U.S. or a rotation base for overseas and sea-to-shore rotations for military personnel. Thus, the manpower can be designated as military if it is needed to maintain tour lengths and personnel turnover at appropriate levels, and should be determined by occupational specialty and based on assignment, rotation and career development policies. Similarly, manpower can be designated as civilian and exempt from private-sector performance if it is needed to maintain civilian overseas tour lengths and turnover at appropriate levels.

Career Progression

Manpower authorities are also required to provide reasonable opportunities for the development of military and civilian personnel. Thus, manpower must be designated as civilian, even if it could be performed by the private sector, if it is needed to provide adequate career paths and progression opportunities, and the day-to-day experiences and skills needed to produce competent leaders, administrators, and personnel with skills that are unique to DoD. Thus, the career progression must be into civilian positions that require technical or leadership skills that cannot be taught or directly acquired from the private sector.

Similarly, manpower should be designated at military in commercial activities in the infrastructure that do not otherwise require military personnel, if it is needed to provide career paths to develop military-unique competencies. Thus, this manpower is designated as military if it is need to provide developmental assignments and day-to-day work experiences necessary to produce military leaders and develop military-unique knowledge and skills.

Law, Executive Order, Treaty, International Agreement

Some activities and tasks are exempted from performance by contractors because of laws, executive orders, and other legal restrictions. For example, depot-level maintenance and repair functions that are not inherently governmental may be exempted from private-sector performance by law or executive order because they help ensure a core logistics capability in the government. Some activities are exempted because of legal restrictions on using contractors or using U.S. or foreign national civilians. Alternatively, some activities may be exempted because they are designated as foreign national civilian, by treaty or international agreement, or because it is impractical to convert these activities from foreign national support.

Management Decision

Management decision is the final criterion, and is the appropriate criterion, if criteria A–L do not apply. Manpower authorities can exempt activities and tasks from private sector performance if sufficient documentation exists to support the decision. For example, analysis might indicate that contractor capability does not exist, because the location is remote, or because an economic analysis indicates that it is more cost-effective to perform the activity or task with military or civilian personnel. Activities or tasks may receive this exemption while they are under review and pending a decision, or until the decision is reviewed.

Qualitative Analysis Approach

As described in Chapter Four, we conducted interviews throughout NSA/CSS as well as within DoD and ODNI. This appendix describes our qualitative approach and provides a copy of the interview protocol we developed to guide the interviews.

With the assistance of NSA/CSS's Senior Language Authority, RAND conducted numerous interviews within DoD and NSA/CSS.[1] The interviews covered several broad groups:

- *Force provider managers:* The managers within each service, within NSA/CSS, and within OSD and ODNI concerned with the supply of language capability and personnel to the national security community and with the career management of these personnel, including hiring, training, promoting, and compensating them.
- Force users or product lines within NSA/CSS: NSA/CSS has an array of product lines that require language capability to complete their missions. We interviewed managers of these product lines.
- *Language trainers:* Much of the language training for the IC and NSA/CSS specifically occurs at the DLIFLC and at the National Cryptologic School. We interviewed managers and instructors at each of these institutions.
- *Language professionals who supply language capability:* The senior language authority at NSA/CSS arranged interviews with groups of employees at each of its three cryptologic centers. These groups included a mix of military and civilian language professionals. In addition, we interviewed managers at each site of these personnel.

We conducted interviews at each of NSA/CSS's three cryptological centers across the United States, as well as at NSA/CSS headquarters at Fort Meade. We conducted interviews with human resource managers concerned with hiring, training, and managing the careers of language professionals at NSA/CSS as well as within each of the service branches and the Office of the Secretary of Defense. Furthermore, we conducted interviews with professionals involved in the language training of linguists including individuals at the DLIFLC, the National Cryptologic School in the Washington D.C. area, and training facilities at the different cryptological centers. While our interviews were quite extensive, we did not visit every NSA/CSS site in the United States or any sites abroad.

To guide the interviews, we developed an interview protocol based on the factors that our framework and DoD instructions indicate are important in determining workforce mixes (dis-

---

[1] The interview protocol and qualitative research approach received Institutional Review Board (IRB) clearance from RAND's Human Subjects Protection Committee.

cussed in Chapters Two and Three). The questionnaire also seeks information on the context in which language professionals are used and the nature of the work they perform. The questionnaire was sent to each individual and group we interviewed prior to our meeting.

The interview questionnaire is shown below. The questionnaire covers four broad areas. The first is the nature of work conducted by language professionals at NSA. This part of the questionnaire focused on the missions, how mission readiness is defined and how language contributes to readiness, the required level of language capability needed for the mission, whether aspects of the work are inherently governmental, collateral responsibilities such as deployment, collateral skills required for the job, and entry and retention standards.

The second broad area focuses on the mix and characteristics of the current workforce that provides language capabilities. This section of the interview protocol requests information about how mix varies by job; how personnel differ in terms of age, stage of career, national origin, aptitude and language capability, and other characteristics; whether these characteristics differ across personnel type; how well matched personnel characteristics are with job requirements; and whether organizations and functional managers have flexibility in how they use different categories of personnel.

The third broad area focuses on gaining information on the factors that explain the current mix of personnel types, including specific policies and practices, budgetary and other constraints, and collateral duties and skills. This third section also requests information on whether individuals believe a different mix would be better to meet the organization's needs and what factors are considered in determining the benefits or limitations of different categories of personnel. Finally, it requests information on what changes in policy and practices would help improve the management of or the mix of personnel.

The final broad area focuses on the policies, practices, and costs of different personnel categories. It requests information on the factors affecting the relative productivity and costs of different categories of personnel, including how long it takes to train different categories in language, how long they stay, and the costs of recruiting, paying, training, and retaining personnel. This fourth section also solicits information on obstacles to performing the language mission for different personnel types, perceptions of the relative cost-effectiveness of different personnel, and how different practices and policies affect the capability and cost of using different categories of personnel.

In general, the questionnaire was intended to guide the discussions and give individuals a clearer idea of our areas of interest. We did not seek responses to every question from each individual we interviewed, so that we could explore in more depth specific issues that were raised by interviewees that they considered particularly relevant. Thus, not every interviewee provided responses to every question. That said, some individuals provided written responses to each question, and their written responses were incorporated in the summary of our findings. In general, our goal in each interview was to ensure that individuals had an opportunity to communicate to us any key issues or input they felt were relevant and important for our study's objectives.

We prepared written notes from our interviews and compiled and organized them according to the major topics in the protocol. The compiled notes were then analyzed qualitatively to identify major themes. The major themes are described in Chapter Four.

Determining the Optimal Mix of Personnel to Provide Language Capability to the Intelligence Community

RAND CORPORATION

Background

The ODNI has commissioned a study by the RAND Corporation on determining the optimal mix of military, civilian, and contract personnel in the intelligence language field.

Because NSA/CSS has by far the largest military and civilian population of language analysts in the intelligence community, as well as a substantial number of contractors, ODNI has directed that the cryptologic community be the subject of the study.

RAND will be analyzing personnel and operational databases as part of their study. To supplement the data analysis as well as assist in the interpretation of findings, RAND is also interviewing individuals who can speak authoritatively on language capability in the Intelligence Community and on the personnel, civilians, military, and contractors, who provide that capability.

The question underlying this study is not "why did NSA/CSS make the decisions to distribute the workforce as it is?" because no individual made the decision: the distribution was inherited and modified over generations. The question being asked is: why should NSA/CSS maintain or change the current makeup? WHAT IS THE OPTIMAL MIX and how do we determine it?

A superficial analysis has already been done of the cost of military initial training and relatively low first term retention relative to the longer careers of civilians. This has suggested to some a compelling reason to change the mix of military and civilian personnel. The purpose of this current RAND study is to examine the cost, ROI, benefit, and other factors relating to the relationship between our work and our workforce, and to provide decisionmakers the definition and data they need to determine the optimal mix.

Interviews

The purpose of the interviews is to develop understanding of the nature of the jobs and assignments that require language capability, and identify and examine factors that impact decisions about the benefits, costs, and optimal mix of military, government civilian, and/or contractor personnel to fill those jobs or assignments. Participation in the interviews is voluntary and the identities of participants and their offices will not be reported.

The issues addressed below are broad and comprehensive; specific questions will be tailored to various audiences based on the role they play in staffing and/or utilizing cryptologic expertise.

Please feel free to raise any important factor that may have been overlooked.

A. Nature of the work

1. What is the scope and nature of the work of different language jobs within the cryptologic community?

   Probe: What does your organization oversee and manage?

2. How do you define mission readiness, and how does language contribute to meeting readiness?

3. What skills are needed to do each job (e.g. analytical, computer technology)?

4. What level of language proficiency is needed to do each job? What language skills do they use on the job (listening, reading, translating, interpreting, analyzing)?

5. Are there aspects of the work performed in the cryptolinguist area that are not "inherently governmental"? Alternatively, is there any work potentially suitable to be performed by contractors?

6. Do personnel deploy for their job? If so, how frequently do they deploy and for how long? Is it hazardous? What language skills are used during deployment? What restrictions are there on particular personnel in particular deployment types?

7. What are the entry and retention standards for each job type with respect to:

    a. citizenship
    b. security clearance
    c. language ability
    d. physical standards
    e. aptitude
    f. other.

B. Mix and characteristics of personnel that provide language capability

1. Across the cryptologic community, what categories of personnel fill the need for language capability (approximate percentages if known)?

    a. Government civilian
    b. Contractor
    c. Military: Active vs. Reserve Component, and by service branch.

2. Does the mix of personnel types differ by type of job discussed above? If so, please describe how.

3. In general, how would you describe the characteristics of those in each category (government civilian, military, contractor) in terms of age, stage of career, gender, aptitude, national origin, language capability coming in? Do they vary by job?

    Probe: Profile the personnel in your organization who provide cryptologic expertise, overall and specifically for those individuals assigned to NSA.

4. Are there characteristics of military personnel that enhance language capability and/ or improve mission effectiveness that are unique to military personnel? How do these characteristics vary by service? What about civilian personnel? Contractors?

5. How consistent is the match between the requirements of the operational positions or job and the qualifications of the personnel (from highly consistent to highly inconsistent) on entry, following initial language and/or cryptologic training, and after an initial operational assignment (e.g. after about three years on the job)? Does consistency differ by category? What explains any inconsistencies?

6. How much flexibility does your organization have in how you use each category of personnel (e.g. ability to work overtime or deploy)? What explains the difference in flexibility?

C. Factors that explain current outcomes with regard to personnel mix

1. Overall, do you see any prominent factors, policies, or practices that you believe explain the current mix of personnel types within the organization?

2. Are there situations in which constraints dictate the choice of personnel types, e.g., mission, technology, operational environment, unique knowledge and skills, budgetary considerations?

3. Do military and civilian rotation and assignment policies affect the availability of needed personnel? How do these policies affect mission-related professional development, improvement of language proficiency, and development of target expertise?

    Probe: Do you have an overall plan for managing assignment and rotation of cryptologic personnel? How are its objectives and how does it work? What priorities do you seek to address? What constraints do you face? How does an assignment at NSA fit into this?

4. How do collateral duties or functions affect the individual's language mission readiness or language mission performance?

    Probe: What aspects of assignments degrade language expertise? Do the use of other skills, such as technical expertise, analytical skills, and other occupation-related skills enhance or degrade language skills?

5. Do you believe a different mix of personnel categories would better fill the organization's needs? If so, why?

    Probe: What alternatives, if any, have you considered in how you develop and source cryptologic capability? When is it essential that this expertise be military and why? Under what circumstances do you think that use of civilians or contractors might be appropriate within your organization?

6. What factors does your component consider in determining the benefits or limitations of the various categories of personnel? How great a value does your component place on these factors (this will help in comparing different component attitudes toward various factors)? What is the effect of these factors on performing the language mission? For example:

    a. Leadership or supervisory development

    b. Flexibility in range of assignments

    c. Ability to fill operational needs other than language analysis.

7. What are obstacles or constraints to maintaining optimal mix, or obtaining a more desired mix (e.g. shortage of supply, costs, constraints on recruiting or hiring, personnel ceilings or billet limits, space or equipment or other support limits)?

8. What changes in policies and practices would you suggest to improve the management of or shape the supply or mix of personnel?

D. Policies, practices, and costs associated with different personnel categories

1. How would you rate the relative productivity of the different categories of personnel (military (by service), civilian, contractor)?

2. When a vacancy occurs, what factors influence how it is filled (short and long run)?

3. How are the different categories recruited? How could more be recruited and what are the main obstacles?

4. For each category, how long do personnel continue doing operational language work? What is the typical career path? What policies, practices, and incentives affect their retention in performing language missions? Are there alternate opportunities for employment that affect their choice to stay or leave language work or to change employment category (government civilian, military, contractor)?

    Probe: Describe career paths within your organization with respect to opportunities to utilize language skills, available incentives, policies governing promotion, retention, and movement within the organization.

5. How are personnel in the different categories trained in language? Are there different paths within each category? How much and what sort of training do they require?

6. What is the cost of recruiting, paying, training, and retaining personnel in each category? What are the cost components and costs in the initial phase (prior to initial operational assignment), and over the time the individual is expected to do operational language work? What portion of the costs is paid for within the intelligence budget (MIP or NIP)?

7. At a given assignment, what percentage of work time is devoted directly to performing the cryptologic language mission for each of the categories?

8. How do you rate the cost-effectiveness of recruiting and maintaining each category of personnel (civilian, military, contractor), considering such factors as total cost, capabilities, length of time devoted to language work in an average workweek, length of time devoted to language work in a typical career, suitability and availability for other intelligence work (e.g. in a follow-on career stage), etc.?

9. At the operational assignment, who (what organizational level and relation to the actual language job) makes decisions regarding assignment, utilization, training, and retention of language personnel in each category in your organization? How do the different practices and policies affect the capability of the language population?

10. How does their perception of relevance or return on investment affect supervisor support for training military or civilian language analysts?

11. Assuming that all will need training throughout a career, what obstacles are there to obtaining it and what is the effect of those obstacles on the ability of the personnel to perform the cryptologic language mission? Are those patterns of causes and effects characteristic of one personnel category or another?

Quantitative Research Approach

Assessing the best mix of military versus civilian personnel to provide language capability to a given IC function requires estimates of the cost and the effectiveness of alternative mixes for that specific IC function and choosing the mix that yields the greatest effect for a given cost or, alternatively, the lowest cost for a given level of effectiveness. We conducted an exploratory assessment of cost and capability of military versus civilian language professionals by developing a spreadsheet inventory projection model. The assessment is exploratory because we do not use data specific to the IC or to the language community, although we do use data on DoD enlisted personnel and on DoD General Schedule (GS) employees, and we are able to use continuation data for cryptologic linguists. Furthermore, the model focuses on what can be measured, namely, expected work years and language proficiency, and not the myriad of other factors that the conceptual framework identifies as potentially important in determining cost and effectiveness. In short, the model can be considered a first look at the relative cost of a military versus civilian linguist workforce. We reiterate that because there are a number of factors that affect cost and effectiveness that are not included in the spreadsheet model, the analysis is just one piece of information that needs to be considered in the workforce mix decision. This appendix describes our methodology in detail with results presented in Chapter Five.

The exploratory model considers two alternative workforces: a military workforce that includes veteran civilians and a comparison workforce consisting only of civilians who have no prior military experience, i.e., nonveterans. Defining the military workforce in this way captures the work generated by enlisted personnel over their entire careers, including their civilian employment. In reality, a civilian workforce would include both veterans and nonveterans. But, if we included the contributions of veterans in our comparison group, we would also have to include their contributions while they were enlisted as well, which would mean that the comparison group would be similar to the military workforce, so we would expect cost differences to be quite small.[1] To highlight the differences, we consider a purely nonveteran workforce as the comparison group. As we explain later, we compute the difference in cost of the military workforce relative to the comparison workforce. Similarities in the contributions of each workforce are netted out. Consequently, our computation of relative cost-effectiveness only considers the marginal or additional contributions of veterans relative to nonveteran civil-

---

[1] Exploratory analysis indicates that this was in fact the case. That is, when we considered the case where the comparison civilian workforce includes veteran and nonveteran civilians as well as the contributions of military personnel (who feed the flow of veteran civilians), the net differences in cost of providing a given level of proficiency are smaller than shown in Table 5.2. Still, the results are qualitatively the same: The comparison workforce is still more cost-effective than the military one. That the net differences are smaller is not surprising given that the compositions of the two workforces are more similar in this alternative comparison.

ians. As we discuss later in this appendix, veterans are assumed to enter the civil service at a higher level of proficiency, but their advantage is temporary.[2]

The model involves two major steps. The first step computes the total expected work years provided by each workforce, adjusted for language proficiency capability. In the process, it also computes the number of accessions of each type of personnel (enlisted personnel, veteran civilians, and nonveteran civilians) required to sustain each workforce as well as the unadjusted expected number of each type of personnel. In the second step, the model uses cost information to compute the total cost of each workforce and the total cost per expected adjusted work year for each workforce. Finally, it computes the difference between the workforces in total cost per expected proficiency-adjusted work year. The latter figure provides information on the relative cost per work year of the military versus the nonveteran civilian workforce.

Tables C.1 and C.2 show the inputs and outputs of the model for the first step of computing expected proficient work years for the civilian workforce and military workforce. We start with an assumed proficient workforce of language professions providing language capability to a given IC mission. We arbitrarily assume this workforce is equal to 2,000 proficient work years. This is seen in the last (right-most) column of Tables C.1 and C.2. For the civilian workforce, P_c, the 2,000 work years are provided by nonveterans ($P_c = 2,000$). For the military workforce, P_m, the 2,000 work years are provided by enlisted personnel, P_e, and civilians who are former military personnel, P_v ($P_m = P_e + P_v$).

The model solves for P_c, P_v, P_e and therefore P_c and P_m as elements of the model's output. For the nonveteran civilian workforce, P_c can be computed given information for nonveteran civilians on continuation behavior and the relationship between proficiency and experience. For the military workforce, we need to compute both P_v and P_e. We compute P_v in the same general way as computed P_c, except we also use information on the fraction of civilian accessions that are veteran. We compute P_e for enlisted personnel, given information on continuation behavior and the relationship between proficiency and experience. In the process, the model also computes the number of enlisted accessions that are needed to sustain P_e, the size of the enlisted workforce (not adjusted for proficiency), as well as the number of civilian acces-

Table C.1
Model Inputs and Outputs for Computing Proficiency-Adjusted Workforce Contributions of the (Nonveteran) Civilian Workforce

Nonveteran Civilians		Total Civilian Workforce
Input	Output	Output
Civilian continuation rates by YOS	Civilian accessions without prior military experience	Total civilian accessions to sustain $P_c = 2,000$
Relationship between proficiency and experience	Proficient workforce of size P_n of nonveteran civilians	Total proficient workforce of size $P_c = 2,000$
Percentage of total civilian accessions that are nonveteran		

---

[2] We could also include the contributions of nonveterans to the military workforce, but since their contributions would be entirely netted out when compared with the nonveteran civilian workforce, we exclude them.

Table C.2
Schematic of Approach to Computing Proficiency-Adjusted Workforce Contributions of Military Workforce

Enlisted Personnel		Veteran Civilians		Total Military Workforce (Enlisted Personnel + Veteran Civilians)
Input	Output	Input	Output	Output
Enlisted continuation rates by YOS	Enlisted accessions to sustain proficient workforce of size P_e	Civilian continuation rates by YOS	Civilian accessions with prior military experience	
Relationship between proficiency and experience	Proficient enlisted workforce of size P_e	Relationship between proficiency and experience for veterans	Proficient workforce of size P_v of nonveteran civilians	Total proficient workforce of size $P_m = P_e + P_v = 2{,}000$
		Percentage of total civilian accessions that are veteran		
		Percentage of military separations and retirements that become a civilian (veteran) accession		

sions required to sustain P_v and P_c and the respective size of the unadjusted veteran and nonveteran civilian workforces.

To make these computations, we require information on continuation rates, the relationship between language proficiency and experience, and the percentage of civilian accessions that are former military personnel. The next subsections describe these inputs. We first consider the workforce contributions of enlisted personnel while in the military, then the contributions the nonveteran civilian workforce and the veteran civilian workforce.

Computing the Proficient Work Years of Enlisted Personnel While in the Military

In general, the contribution of a workforce to proficiency, measured as the number of proficient work years, is computed by first computing the number of work years provided by a source of personnel, W, and then adjusting those years for the amount of proficiency, P. This subsection describes specifically how we compute P_e.

We compute work years provided by enlisted while they are in the military, W_e, using historical continuation rates for enlisted personnel together with input on enlisted accessions. Historical continuation rates by YOS for enlisted personnel who are in cryptologic linguist occupations were obtained for FY 2000–2009 from the DMDC, and we used the average across these fiscal years by YOS, shown in Figure C.1. These continuation rates imply an average number of work years per accession of 4.6 years, a figure that is lower than the average number for all enlisted personnel over the same period. The continuation rates we use are based on continuation within the cryptologic linguist field. Thus, if a member in this field stays in the military but changes occupation out of this field, it would be considered a separation for

Figure C.1
Average Year-to-Year Continuation Rates Within the Cryptologic Linguist Occupations, by Year of Service, Cryptologic Linguist Enlisted Personnel (All Services), FY 2000–2009

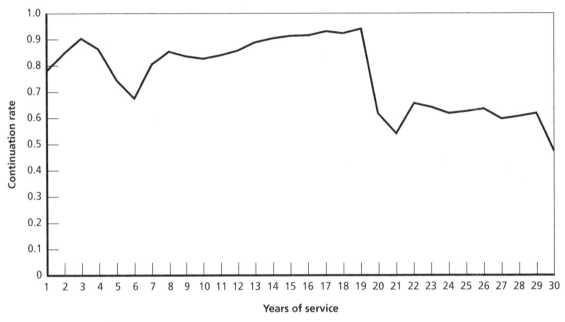

SOURCE: Defense Manpower Data System, Information Delivery System.
RAND *TR1284-C.1*

this calculation. Using continuation rates that do not consider whether a member stays in this field (i.e., a member who changes field is still considered to be in the military) does not change the results much. Under this assumption, the average work years per accession are 4.9 years. Thus, relatively few cryptologic linguists change fields while in the military over the period we consider.

The next step is to adjust work years for amount of proficiency provided. This adjustment requires information on how language proficiency varies with experience. Language proficiency is assessed in DoD based on the results of the DLPT, a test developed by the Defense Language Institute of DoD. The DLPT assesses general proficiency of native English speakers in foreign languages across two dimensions: listening and reading comprehension. DLPT scores are stated in levels for each, ranging from 0+ through 3 or 4 in listening and reading, respectively. For example, a test result of 2/2 indicates that the test taker is rated as "limited working proficiency" in each area (U.S. Coast Guard, Training Center Cape May, 2012).

Our interviews, described in Chapter Four, indicated that language proficiency, and specifically DLPT scores, are an imperfect measure of language capability to perform a given mission because they focus on testing global language skills rather than skills required to perform a specific mission. Unfortunately, DLPT scores are the best available source of information until better metrics are found. We assumed a relationship between proficiency and experience based on input we received from our interviews.

We heard in interviews that because of training, including basic training, language training, and cryptologic training, enlisted language personnel generally do not become qualified for their occupational specialty until mid-way or even the end of their second year of service.

We assume that military personnel are available to provide proficient work to meet mission requirements at YOS 3. Prior to then, we assume they provide no productive work to the language mission under consideration. We assume that at YOS 3, they have a proficiency of 2/2 in listening and reading, based on input from DLIFLC that language training seeks to train personnel to this level. Based on interview input that personnel do not achieve full proficiency until they reach YOS 8, we assume that enlisted personnel reach the level of 3/3 by YOS 8, whereupon we assume they maintain this level the rest of their enlisted career, assuming they stay.

We normalize proficiency at the beginning of YOS 3 (when enlisted complete their training, by assumption) as equal to 1, representing a proficiency of 2/2. We assume proficiency grows linearly between YOS 3 and 8 to a value of 1.2. This approach implicitly assumes that a level of 3/3 represents a 20 percent higher level of proficiency. Thus, we create a proficiency index, equal to 1 at YOS 3, rising linearly to 1.2 at YOS 8, and remaining at 1.2 thereafter for the remainder of the career. Our analysis of language proficiency is informed by our interviews but clearly also embeds some arbitrary assumptions. We therefore considered alternative assumptions to ascertain the sensitivity of the results to these assumptions. In general, we find that changing the assumptions does little to affect the difference in cost per proficiency-adjusted work year between military and civilian personnel, though it does change the level of costs of each type of personnel.

For example, we also consider the cases where military personnel contribute to the language mission after their first year in one case and immediately upon entry in a second case, rather than after their second year. We also consider the case (not shown) where after completing training (at the end of their second year), proficiency is 1+/1+ rather than 2/2, grows to 2/2 by YOS 6, and does not grow to 3/3 until much later in the mid-career, around 15 years of service. This latter case allows us to consider the results when we assume a lower level of enlisted proficiency and slower growth over the career.

To compute proficiency-adjusted work years, P_e, for a given enlisted accession, we compute the number of work years contributed in each YOS, given continuation rates by YOS, and adjust that number by the proficiency index. We sum across years of service to obtain the expected proficiency-adjusted work years for a given accession. We multiply this number by the number of accessions.

Computing the Proficiency-Adjusted Workforce Contribution of the Nonveteran Civilian Workforce and the Veteran Civilian Workforce

Computing the total proficiency-adjusted work years of nonveteran and veteran civilian personnel to the language mission, P_c and P_v, respectively, requires information on the number of nonveteran and veteran accessions, on continuation behavior, and on how proficiency grows with experience.

We compute veteran accessions in the base case as equal to half of total civilian accessions. Our interviews revealed that many of civilians providing language capability in the IC are former military personnel. Available data confirms this finding for DoD civilians in general. Gates et al. (2008) finds that in 2006, half of DoD civilian accessions were former military personnel. We use this 50 percent flow rate as our baseline rate. In cases 4 and 5, we consider alternative assumptions: case 4, in which no civilians are veterans and there is no flow of veterans to the civil service, case 5, in which 75 percent of civilians are veterans and 32 percent of veterans join the civil service. In unpublished work, Rostker finds that between 2004 and 2006, 8 percent of enlisted personnel who served in enlisted intelligence occupations and were separated or retired from active duty were hired as civilians. We incorporate this finding into the model by assuming in the base case that civilian veteran accessions are 8 percent of enlisted separations and retirements in the model over a three-year period. In case 4, this figure is 0 percent, and in case 5, this figure is 32 percent.

For a given civilian accession, we can compute expected work years unadjusted for proficiency using information on continuation rates in the DoD civil service. Unfortunately, we do not have continuation rates for veteran versus nonveteran civilians, so we assume the same continuation behavior for both groups. Figure C.2, adapted from Figure 3.11 in Gates et al. (2008), shows the voluntary and involuntary separation rates for all DoD civilian employees with a bachelor's degree for 2005–2006. Continuation rates are equal to 100 percent minus separation rates. Because we only have rates by YOS, we use the same rate for each YOS in each category. For example, for YOSs 0–4, we use a continuation rate of 91 percent. These continuation rates imply an average of 14.1 work years per accession for the DoD civilian workforce.

We next must adjust expected work years for language proficiency. As with military personnel, language proficiency scores are an imperfect measure of language capability to perform a given mission, according to the people we interviewed. We assumed a relationship between proficiency and experience based on input we received from our interviews. We assume that civilians are available to provide proficient work to meet mission requirements immediately as soon as they are hired.

We consider two alternative indices of proficiency-experience profiles for civilians. First, we consider the case where the civilian proficiency index by YOS is identical to the one we use for enlisted personnel, i.e., we assume proficiency grows in an identical fashion to military per-

Figure C.2
Voluntary and Involuntary Separation Rates for DoD Civilians with Bachelor's Degrees, 2005–2006

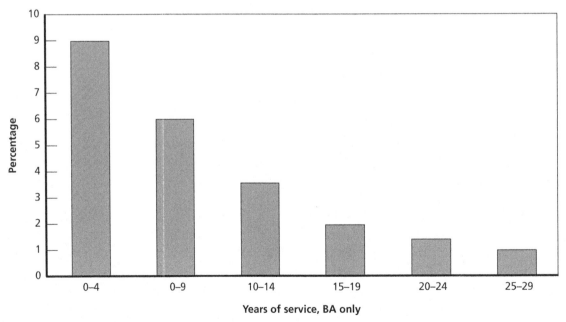

SOURCE: Adapted from Gates et al. (2008), Figure 3.11.

RAND *TR1284-C.2*

sonnel, with the exception that proficient work starts at entry, rather than in YOS 3. For the nonveteran civilian personnel, this means that the index equals 1 at YOS 1. For veteran civilian personnel, we assume that their proficiency at entry is equal to that of an enlisted member after five years of service. This is based on the fact that the expected years of service for a cryptologic linguist is 4.6 years (or five, rounding up). Put differently, we recognize that civilians with prior military experience gain proficiency while they are in the military, and we assign them a level of proficiency at entry to the civil service equal to the index value at the expected years of service for an enlisted member (or five). Thus, veteran civilians enter civilian service with a proficiency index of 1.12 rather than 1, because 1.12 is the value of the proficiency index for military personnel at YOS 6 (e.g., after five years of service).

Thus, in the first case, we assume the nonveteran civilian personnel enter with a DLPT proficiency of 2/2 for listening and reading, corresponding to an index of 1, growing uniformly to 3/3, which corresponds to an index of 1.2, by YOS 6, whereupon they maintain a 3/3 proficiency for the remainder of their civilian career.[3] For the veteran civilian workforce, we assume they enter at YOS 1 in the civil service with an index of 1.12, growing to 1.2 by YOS 3 and remaining at that level thereafter. Thus, veterans have an advantage over nonveterans in terms of their contribution to proficiency, since they enter at an index level of 1.12 rather than 1. However, the advantage is temporary, since nonveterans catch up by YOS 6. Furthermore, because our computation of relative cost-effectiveness is based on cost differences, only the marginal or additional advantage of veterans is included, and, as mentioned, this advantage is transient. These profiles are the ones assumed for the results shown in Table 5.1 in Chapter Five.

In the second case, we assume that both veteran and nonveteran civilians have a higher level of proficiency, consistent with what we heard in interviews. In this case, we assume civilians enter with DLPT scores of 3/3 for listening and reading proficiency, regardless of their veteran's status, and that they maintain this level their entire career. In this case, the proficiency index starts at 1.2 at YOS 1 for both veterans and nonveterans and remains at that level the remainder of the career. We find that our results differ a bit across the two cases, but not by much (not shown). Thus, the results in Chapter Five are robust to a different assumption about civilian language proficiency.

To compute proficiency-adjusted work years for a given veteran or nonveteran civilian accession, we compute the number of work years contributed in each year of service, given continuation rates by year of service, and adjust the number of years by the appropriate proficiency index (for veterans versus nonveterans). We sum across years of service to compute expected proficiency-adjusted work years for each group.

Computing the Expected Total Contribution of Civilians

Given the contributions of nonveteran civilians, the total workforce proficiency-adjusted contribution of civilians is $P_c = 2,000$, by assumption. This assumption, together with the methodology described in the previous subsection on how we compute P_c, allows us to solve for the total number of civilian accessions required to sustain P_c. In the process, the model also

---

[3] Unlike military personnel, language proficiency is currently not measured by DLPT scores but by other assessment tools. Since proficiency in the model is based on an assumed relationship, we measure proficiency in terms of DLPT for civilians and military personnel.

computes the size of the nonveteran civilian workforce, unadjusted for proficiency. This figure is required for computing cost, described later in this appendix.

Computing the Expected Total Contribution of Military Personnel Over the Enlisted Career

The expected total contribution of military personnel, P_m, equals their expected contribution while they are in the military, P_e, plus their expected contribution in the civil service (accounting for the likelihood of joining the civil service), P_v. By assumption, $P_m = P_e + P_v = 2,000$. Given the computation of P_v and the methodology for computing P_e, described earlier in this appendix, the model computes the number of enlisted accessions required to sustain a force of P_e, given that $P_e + P_v = 2,000$. In the process, the model also computes the size of the enlisted workforce, not adjusted for proficiency, a piece of information required for computing cost.

It should be clear that the computations shown in Table C.2 of the expected contributions of enlisted and veteran civilian personnel are performed jointly, though described here separately. The model is an Excel-based workbook that embeds these computations.

Computing Cost

Chapter Three describes the cost elements stipulated in DoD DTM 09-007 for estimating and comparing the full cost to the government of military versus civilian manpower, shown in Figure 3.1. The memorandum not only lists the elements but provides the websites that yield the data for estimating these elements. We accessed these websites and used the cost elements for FY 2011, with the exception of two key cost elements for military language professions, training costs and recruitment costs. For military personnel, we use cost elements for all enlisted personnel, not specifically language personnel, as referenced in DTM 09-007, but excluded training and recruitment costs. Excluding training and recruitment costs, the average cost per work year of an enlisted member is $102,090.

We use a different training cost estimate than the one referenced in DTM 09-007, because training costs for language training can be quite high relative to the average, as discussed below. We use a different recruitment estimate, because we vary recruitment costs in case 3 to include an enlistment bonus associated with recruiting more proficient enlistees.

Total training costs (entry, initial occupational-related, career) averaged across all enlisted personnel (not just accessions or trainees) in FY11 are $1,158, according to DoD budget figures. A rough calculation, assuming an enlisted strength of 1.2 million and annual enlisted accessions of 175,000, implies a cost of about $7,900 per accession. This figure is very low relative to other information about training costs, especially for language personnel.

Information from DLIFLC indicates that average language-training cost per graduate for an enlisted member can be quite high, especially for languages requiring long training times, such as Arabic or Chinese. For example, average training cost per graduate can be as high as $200,000 per enlisted graduate of DLIFLC, and costs will vary with language and enlisted grade. Assuming that about half of accessions in language-related occupations eventually graduate from language training (a figure mentioned repeatedly during our interviews), this would suggest that the average cost per accession of training a recruit in a difficult language is about $100,000. This figure does not include the cost of basic training or specialized skills training, such as training to become a cryptologic linguist. Training cost data are difficult to find, but information available from the Army's recruiting website (U.S. Army Recruiting Command, 2011) indicates that the average cost of training a new recruit in 2010 (including recruiting costs) was $73,000. The Army recruiting website also reports an average recruitment cost of about $20,000, so the net training cost of basic training and advanced individual (skills) training is $53,000. Thus, a rough estimate of training cost per recruit including training in a difficult language would be about $153,000 ($53,000 + $100,000). This figure is well in excess of the enlisted average of $7,900.

For our analysis, we assume an average training cost per enlisted accession of $100,000, a very conservative estimate of training costs. We chose a figure lower than the $153,000 because of our uncertainty about actual training costs and because a lower training cost assumption favors military personnel. In case 2, when we consider the situation of language training being reduced by 1 year, we lower this figure to $75,000 per accession, and in case 3, when we consider the situation of language training being all but eliminated because new recruits are already proficient in a language, we reduce this figure to $50,000. Training costs are still relatively high even with proficient recruits because of the cost of basic training and initial skill training.

Average recruitment costs per accession were obtained from the Office of Accession Policy within the Office of the Secretary of Defense for Personnel and Readiness. We averaged these costs over the period 2007 to 2011 in real 2011 dollars for a figure of $19,600, similar to the figure reported on the Army recruiting website of $20,000. For simplicity, we rounded this figure to $20,000 per enlisted accession. In case 3, when we assume the military offers bonuses to attract more proficient recruits, we increase this figure to $40,000. Thus, in case 3, training costs are lower, equal to $50,000, but recruitment costs are higher, equal to $40,000, given our assumptions.

To compute the cost of an enlisted workforce, we multiply the size of the (proficiency-unadjusted) workforce by $102,090 and multiply the number accession by the recruitment cost per accession and by the training cost per accession. The total is the cost of the enlisted workforce required to sustain P_e.

Next, we compute the costs of the veteran and nonveteran civilian workforces. We use the cost elements listed in DTM 09-007 and in Table 3.1. For FY 2011, the average cost of a DoD civilian was $111,056. To compute the cost of the veteran civilian workforce, we multiply this average cost figure by the size of the veteran civilian workforce required to sustain P_v, and similarly, to compute the cost of the nonveteran civilian workforce we multiply this figure by the size of the nonveteran workforce required to sustain P_c.

The average cost of $111,056 is assumed to be the same for veterans and nonveterans, though the costs of the veteran and nonveteran workforces are not equal because P_v and P_c are not equal.

Bibliography

About.com—U.S. Military, "Air Force Enlisted Job Descriptions: 1N3XX—Cryptologic Linguist," no date. As of August 22, 2012:
http://usmilitary.about.com/od/airforceenlistedjobs/a/afjob1n3x1.htm

Alchian, Armen, and Harold Demsetz, "Production, Information Costs, and Economic Organization," *American Economic Review*, Vol. 62, No. 5, 1972, pp. 777–795.

Asch, Beth J., "The Economic Complexities of Incentive Reforms," in Robert Klitgaard and Paul C. Light, eds., *High-Performance Government: Structure, Leadership, Incentives*, Santa Monica, Calif.: RAND Corporation, MG-256-PRGS, 2005, pp. 309–343. As of August 17, 2012:
http://www.rand.org/pubs/monographs/MG256.html

Asch, Beth J., Dina G. Levy, and Heather Krull, "The Retention and Career Paths of Military Intelligence Linguists: Interim Findings," Santa Monica, Calif.: RAND Corporation, unpublished manuscript, 2009.

Asch, Beth J., and John T. Warner, "A Theory of Compensation and Personnel Policy in Hierarchical Organizations with Application to the United States Military," *Journal of Labor Economics*, Vol. 19, No. 3, July 2001, pp. 523–562.

Berteau, David, Joachim Hofbauer, Jesse Ellman, Gregory Kiley, and Guy Ben-Ari, *DoD Workforce Cost Realism Assessment*, Washington, D.C.: Center for Strategic and International Studies, May 2011.

Borjas, George, *Labor Economics, Third Edition*, Boston, Mass.: McGraw-Hill Irwin, 2005.

Builder, Carl H., *The Masks of War: American Military Styles in Strategy and Analysis*, Baltimore: Johns Hopkins University Press, 1989.

Burgess, Simon, and Marisa Ratto, "The Role of Incentives in the Public Sector: Issues and Evidence," *Oxford Review of Economic Policy*, Vol. 19, No. 2, 2003, pp. 285–300.

Camerer, Colin, and Ari Vepsalainen, "The Economic Efficiency of Corporate Culture," *Strategic Management Journal*, Vol. 9, 1988, pp. 115–126.

Congressional Research Service, *Inherently Governmental Functions and Department of Defense Operations: Background, Issues, and Options for Congress*, R40641, July 2009. As of August 29, 2012:
http://www.fas.org/sgp/crs/misc/R40641.pdf.

Dahlman, Carl J., *The Cost of a Military Person-Year: A Method for Computing Savings from Force Reductions*, Santa Monica, Calif.: RAND Corporation, MG-598-OSD, 2007. As of August 17, 2012:
http://www.rand.org/pubs/monographs/MG598.html

Defense Language Institute Foreign Language Center, "Defense Language Institute Foreign Language Center (DLIFLC) Defense Language Proficiency Test (DLPT) Program," 2007.

Demsetz, Harold, "The Theory of the Firm Revisited," *Journal of Law, Economics, and Organization*, Vol. 4, No. 1, 1988, pp. 141–161.

DFIFLC—*see* Defense Language Institute Foreign Language Center.

Dixit, Avinash, "Incentives and Organizations in the Public Sector: An Interpretative Review," *Journal of Human Resources*, Vol. 37, No. 4, Autumn 2002, pp. 696–727.

DoD—*see* U.S. Department of Defense.

Gates, Susan M., *Shining a Spotlight on the Defense Acquisition Workforce—Again*, Santa Monica, Calif.: RAND Corporation, OP-266-OSD, 2009. As of August 17, 2012:
http://www.rand.org/pubs/occasional_papers/OP266.html

Gates, Susan M., and Albert A. Robbert, *Comparing the Costs of DoD Military and Civil Service Personnel*, Santa Monica, Calif.: RAND Corporation, MR-980-OSD, 1998. As of August 17, 2012:
http://www.rand.org/pubs/monograph_reports/MR980.html

———, *Personnel Savings in Competitively Sourced DoD Activities: Are They Real? Will They Last?* Santa Monica, Calif.: RAND Corporation, 2000, MR-1117-OSD. As of August 17, 2012:
http://www.rand.org/pubs/monograph_reports/MR1117.html

Gates, Susan M., Edward G. Keating, Adria D. Jewell, Lindsay Daugherty, Bryan Tysinger, Albert A. Robbert, and Ralph Masi, *The Defense Acquisition Workforce: An Analysis of Personnel Trends Relevant to Policy, 1993–2006*. Santa Monica, Calif.: RAND Corporation, TR-572-OSD, 2008. As of August 29, 2012:
http://www.rand.org/pubs/technical_reports/TR572.html

Gotz, Glenn A., Michael G. Shanley, Robert A. Butler, and Barry Fishman, *Estimating the Cost of Changes in the Active/Reserve Balance*, Santa Monica, Calif.: RAND Corporation, R-3748-PA&E/FMP/JCS, 1990. As of August 17, 2012:
http://www.rand.org/pubs/reports/R3748.html

Headquarters, U.S. Department of the Army, *Human Intelligence Collector Operations*, Field Manual 2-22.3, September 2006. As of August 17, 2012:
http://www.enlisted.info/field-manuals/fm-2-22.3-human-intelligence-collector-operations.shtml

———, *Army Foreign Language Program*, Army Regulation 11-6, December 2007. As of August 17, 2012:
http://www.army.mil/usapa/epubs/pdf/r11_6.pdf

Hix, William M., Herbert J. Shukiar, Janet M. Hanley, Richard J. Kaplan, Jennifer H. Kawata, Grant Marshall, and Peter Stan, *Personnel Turbulence: The Policy Determinants of Permanent Change of Station Moves*, Santa Monica, Calif.: RAND Corporation, MR-938-A, 1998. As of August 17, 2012:
http://www.rand.org/pubs/monograph_reports/MR938.html

Holmstrom, Bengt, and Paul Milgrom, "Multi-Task Principal-Agent Analyses: Incentive Contracts, Asset Ownership, and Job Design," *Journal of Law, Economics, and Organization*, Vol. 7, 1991, pp. 24–57.

———, "The Firm as an Incentive System," *American Economic Review*, Vol. 84, No. 4, 1994, pp. 972–991.

ILR—*see* Interagency Language Roundtable.

Interagency Language Roundtable, homepage, no date. As of August 17, 2012:
http://www.govtilr.org/

Jensen, Michael, and William Meckling, "Theory of the Firm: Managerial Behavior, Agency Costs, and Ownership Structure," *Journal of Financial Economics*, Vol. 3, 1976, pp. 305–360.

Klein, Benjamin, Robert Crawford, and Armen Alchian, "Vertical Integration, Appropriable Rents, and the Competitive Contracting Process," *Journal of Law and Economics*, Vol. 21, 1978, pp. 297–326.

Kogut, Bruce, and Udo Zander, "What Firms Do? Coordination, Identity, and Learning," *Organization Science*, Vol. 7, No. 5, 1996, pp. 502–518.

Kreps, David, "Corporate Culture and Economic Theory," in James E. Alt and Kenneth A. Shepsle, eds., *Rational Perspectives on Positive Political Economy*, New York: Cambridge University Press, 1990, pp. 90–143.

Lazear, Edward P., "Corporate Culture and the Diffusion of Values," in Horst Siebert, ed., *Trends in Business Organizations: Do Participation and Cooperation Increase Competitiveness*, Tubingen, Germany: J. C. B. Mohr (Paul Siebeck), 1995, pp. 89–133.

Lazear, Edward P., and Michael Gibbs, *Personnel Economics in Practice*, 2nd edition, New York: John Wiley and Sons, 2009.

Luckey, John, Valerie Bailey Grasso, and Kate Manuel, *Inherently Governmental Functions and Department of Defense Operations: Background, Issues, and Options for Congress*, Washington, D.C.: Congressional Research Service, 7-5700, June 22, 2009. As of August 17, 2012:
http://www.fas.org/sgp/crs/misc/R40641.pdf

Makingthedifference.org, "Foreign Languages Jobs in the Federal Government," no date. As of August 22, 2012:
http://www.makingthedifference.org/federalcareers/foreignlanguage.shtml

National Security Agency/Central Security Service, "Career Fields," 2009a. As of August 22, 2012:
http://www.nsa.gov/careers/career_fields/index.shtml

———, "Career Fields—Foreign Language—Language Analyst," 2009b. As of August 22, 2012:
http://www.nsa.gov/careers/career_fields/foreignlang.shtml

———, "Frequently Asked Questions—Employment/Business Opportunities," 2009c. As of August 22, 2012:
http://www.nsa.gov/about/faqs/opportunities.shtml

———, "Mission," 2009d. As of August 22, 2012:
http://www.nsa.gov/about/mission/index.shtml

NSA/CSS—*see* National Security Agency/Central Security Service.

Palmer, Adele R., James H. Bigelow, Joseph G. Bolton, Deena Dizengoff, Jennifer H. Kawata, Hugh G. Massey, Robert Petruschell, and Michael G. Shanley, *Assessing the Structure and Mix of the Future Active and Reserve Forces: Cost Estimation Methodology*, Santa Monica, Calif.: RAND Corporation, MR-134-1-OSD, 1992. As of August 17, 2012:
http://www.rand.org/pubs/monograph_reports/MR134-1.html

Poppo, Laura, and Todd Zenger, "Alternative Theories of the Firm: Transaction Cost, Knowledge-Based, and Measurement Explanations for the Make-or-Buy Decisions in Information Services," *Strategic Management Journal*, Vol. 19, No. 9, 1998, pp. 853–877.

Porter, Clifford F., "Asymmetrical Warfare, Transformation, and Foreign Language Capability," Ft. Leavenworth, Kan.: U.S. Army Command and General Staff College, Combat Studies Institute, 2006. As of August 17, 2012:
http://www.cgsc.edu/carl/download/csipubs/porter.pdf

Riposo, Jessie, Irv Blickstein, Stephanie Young, Geoffrey McGovern, and Brian McInnis, *An In-Sourcing Assessment for the Navy's Assistant Deputy Chief of Naval Operations for Integration of Capabilities and Resources*, Santa Monica, Calif.: RAND Corporation, TR-944-NAVY, 2011. As of August 17, 2012:
http://www.rand.org/pubs/technical_reports/TR944.html

Robbert, Albert A., William A. Williams, and Cynthia R. Cook, *Principles for Determining the Air Force Active/Reserve Mix*, Santa Monica, Calif.: RAND Corporation, MR-1091-AF, 1999. As of August 17, 2012:
http://www.rand.org/pubs/monograph_reports/MR1091.html

Rostker, Bernard D., *A Call to Revitalize the Engines of Government*, Santa Monica, Calif.: RAND Corporation, OP-240-OSD, 2008. As of August 17, 2012:
http://www.rand.org/pubs/occasional_papers/OP240.html

Stevens, LTC Steve, "Utilizing Linguists on the Battlefield," unpublished briefing, 30th Military Intelligence Brigade Language Conference, March 11, 2007.

U.S. Army, "Cryptologic Linguist (35P)," no date. As of August 22, 2012:
http://www.goarmy.com/careers-and-jobs/browse-career-and-job-categories/intelligence-and-combat-support/cryptologic-linguist.html

U.S. Army Recruiting Command, "Support Army Recruiting," 2011. As of August 23, 2012:
http://www.usarec.army.mil/support/#costper

U.S. Coast Guard, Training Center Cape May, "Defense Language Proficiency Test," 2012. As of August 23, 2012:
http://www.uscg.mil/hq/capemay/education/dlpt.asp

U.S. Department of Defense, *Defense Language Transformation Roadmap*, Washington, D.C., January 2005. As of August 17, 2012:
http://handle.dtic.mil/100.2/ADB313370

————, *Department of Defense Instruction 1100.4: Guidance for Manpower Management*, Office of the Under Secretary of Defense (Personnel and Readiness), Washington, D.C., February 12, 2005.

————, *Memorandum for Assistant Secretaries of the Army (M&RA), Navy (M&RA) and Air Force (M&RA) on Special Pay for Foreign Language Proficiency*, Office of the Under Secretary of Defense (Plans) Senior Language Authority (Gail McGinn), Washington, D.C., February 6, 2006.

————, *Directive-Type Memorandum (DTM) 09-007: Estimating and Comparing the Full Costs of Civilian and Military Manpower and Contract Support*, Office of the Under Secretary of Defense (Cost Assessment and Program Evaluation), Washington, D.C., January 29, 2010.

————, FY 2011 *Department of Defense (DoD) Military Personnel Composite Standard Pay and Reimbursement Rates*, Office of the Under Secretary of Defense (Program/Budget), Washington, D.C., March 24, 2010.

————, *Department of Defense Instruction 1100.22: Guidance for Determining Workforce Mix*, Office of the Under Secretary of Defense (Personnel and Readiness), Washington, D.C., April 12, 2010.

U.S. Government Accountability Office, *GAO Cost Estimating and Assessment Guide*, Washington, D.C., GAO-09-3SP, March 2009.

Webopedia, "Cryptography," no date. As of August 22, 2012:
http://www.webopedia.com/TERM/C/cryptography.html

Warner, John T., *Thinking About Military Retirement*, Alexandria, Va.: Center for Naval Analyses, CRM D0013583.A1/Final, 2006.

Williamson, Oliver, *The Economic Institutions of Capitalism: Firms, Markets, and Relational Contracting*, New York: The Free Press, 1985.

Made in the USA
Coppell, TX
03 November 2022

85719942R00057